TOAST

REAL FOOD FOR

HASH

EVERY TIME OF DAY

ROAST

DAN DOHERTY

MASH

MITCHELL BEAZLEY

AN HACHETTE UK COMPANY
WWW.HACHETTE.CO.UK

FIRST PUBLISHED IN GREAT BRITAIN IN 2016 BY MITCHELL BEAZLEY
A DIVISION OF OCTOPUS PUBLISHING GROUP LTD
CARMELITE HOUSE, 50 VICTORIA EMBANKMENT
LONDON EC4Y 0DZ
WWW.OCTOPUSBOOKS.CO.UK
WWW.OCTOPUSBOOKSUSA.COM

THIS EDITION PUBLISHED IN 2018

DISTRIBUTED IN THE US BY HACHETTE BOOK GROUP
1290 AVENUE OF THE AMERICAS, 4TH AND 5TH FLOORS,
NEW YORK, NY 10104

DISTRIBUTED IN CANADA BY CANADIAN MANDA GROUP
664 ANNETTE ST., TORONTO, ONTARIO, CANADA M6S 2C8

ISBN 978 1 78472 552 5

A CIP CATALOGUE RECORD FOR THIS BOOK IS AVAILABLE FROM
THE BRITISH LIBRARY.

PRINTED AND BOUND IN ITALY
10 9 8 7 6 5 4 3 2 1

PUBLISHER: ALISON STARLING
MANAGING EDITOR: SYBELLA STEPHENS
ART DIRECTOR: JULIETTE NORSWORTHY
DESIGNER: GEOFF FENNELL
PHOTOGRAPHER: ANDERS SCHØNNEMANN
FOOD STYLISTS: DAN DOHERTY & TOM CENCI
PROP STYLIST: LIZ BELTON
SENIOR PRODUCTION MANAGER: KATHERINE HOCKLEY

EGGS SHOULD BE MEDIUM UNLESS OTHERWISE STATED.
THIS BOOK CONTAINS DISHES MADE WITH LIGHTLY COOKED EGGS.
IT IS PRUDENT FOR MORE VULNERABLE PEOPLE SUCH AS PREGNANT
AND NURSING MOTHERS, INVALIDS, THE ELDERLY, BABIES AND
YOUNG CHILDREN TO AVOID UNCOOKED OR LIGHTLY COOKED EGGS.

TOAST
HASH
ROAST
MASH

Contents

Introduction

The kind of food in this book is what I like to cook at home and eat and share with my friends and family. It's relaxed, informal and I promise the recipes are easy to make. At Duck & Waffle, where I work, the food is more intricate. Home is where I just want to chill out and eat good food – I hope the recipes here reflect that philosophy. I was so excited to write this book as I have been cooking the dishes for years, so I'm keen to share some of my favourites with you.

The style

Breakfast and brunch are the two meals that I see people getting most excited about – I wouldn't be surprised if a brunch party is soon to be the new dinner party. With such a diverse range of dishes from culture to culture, the list of brunch options is endless. There are breads with lightly curried vegetables and fried eggs from India, to sweet pastry delicacies from Italy – you can get really creative. Brunch feels relaxed, easy-going and, most importantly, approachable. Nobody has time to prep for three hours for breakfast and some of the best-selling dishes at Duck & Waffle are those that use just four ingredients and take 10 minutes to make. It doesn't all have to be indulgent either; the food can be light and still tasty.

The British tend to have big breakfasts and dinners with smaller lunches, and it makes sense that starch- and protein-based recipes intended for breakfast or dinner are interchangeable. It's a natural thing to crave runny eggs and well-cooked meat in the evening or spiced savoury things for breakfast. A good hash is a great example – leftover roast potatoes from the day before, some bacon, maybe a little onion and a touch of spice. Add a pair of fried eggs and I can't decide if I'd rather eat this in the morning or in the evening.

As well as the breakfast-inspired recipes in this book there are plenty of savoury all-day-style dishes, such as Grilled Sea Trout with Little Gem, Potato and Mustard Salad, or how about a playful riff on a coronation chicken using those familiar flavours with smoked haddock and transforming it into a pie?

There is chapter dedicated to one of my favourite ingredients – eggs. Eggs are a staple in my house and I can easily add them to any dish and any meal. I'm obsessed. There are also chapters on pancakes and toast. The British have this wonderful habit of putting everything on toast and I fully embrace it.

I believe the best state of mind in which to create wonderful food is when you're feeling a little delicate. Yes, I mean hungover. Some of the creations that have come to me have been due to the cravings the morning after the night before. Duck & Waffle's iconic Colombian eggs came from just that – albeit someone else's hangover! These moments have inspired some of the dishes in this book along with my lifestyle – sometimes I'll have dinner at midnight or even at 6am after a night shift. I don't recommend the lifestyle, but the food is pretty good. I hope this translates into the perfect meal for you too.

ON TOAST

1

Whoever decided to toast bread was a genius. It's the perfect vehicle for so many things. The likelihood is, however, that there was no one genius but an evolution of ideas by many people. Like a lot of today's wonderful foods we think it came about as a preservation method.

Around 3000BC, when the Egyptians first created the closed oven, leavened bread left out in the scorching desert heat would dry out and be pretty unpleasant to eat. They discovered that toasting the bread made it last much longer.

The Romans loved toast too. In fact, the word "toast" comes from the Latin word *tostum*, meaning "to burn" or "to scorch". Fires were used back then, and that's probably my preferred method now. Failing that, a good griddle pan and plenty of olive oil does the trick.

Talking of preserving, think about French toast. "Pain perdu" translates as "lost bread". Soaking stale bread in eggs rehydrates it, and after being fried in butter, naturally, makes a bloody good dish. There's a recipe on page 194.

On to the bread itself. My recipes call for sourdough – that's my bread of choice. Why? When toasted it holds the crispiness much better than others, meaning that when your topping goes on it holds firm. Of course, this is just my preference – you can use whichever bread you prefer. Just bear in mind if using a sliced loaf or a light, soft crusted bread: it may go a little soft after being topped.

Jams & marmalades

Jams & marmalades The world of jams and marmalades is a very sticky one indeed. You will find endless recipes, rules and tips in books and online, but don't let that scare you. Here I have written a few of my favourite and, most importantly, some of the easiest recipes that I have come across over the years. There are a few pointers that can't be avoided if you want a jam to be proud of.

Sterilize your jars. This is key to ensuring your jam lasts. Simply simmer your jars in a pan of water for 10 minutes, then let them air dry and you're good to go.

Make sure you dissolve the sugar in the fruit on a low heat before increasing to a high heat to get jammin'. This helps the jam set nicely.

When you're in full jam swing, don't worry about skimming off the foam that will come to the top; wait until you are at jam stage and stir in a knob of butter – that'll get rid of it all.

Once you're comfortable making jams and marmalades, you can have fun using different fruits, inventing combinations, and even adding herbs and spices to change the flavour.

Strawberry jam

Makes 2 x 454g (1lb) jars
Preparation time: 20 minutes
Cooking time: 10 minutes

1kg (2lb 4oz) fresh strawberries, washed, dried and hulled
1kg (2lb 4oz) jam sugar
juice of 1 lemon
15g (½oz) butter

Place a small plate in the freezer for later and have your jars sterilized, ready to go. Toss the strawberries in half the sugar and set aside for 15 minutes.

Put the strawberries into a pan with the lemon juice and the remaining sugar. Gently heat until the sugar is all dissolved (you can test this by dipping a spoon in and seeing if there are any granules of sugar on it). If any sugar is caught on the side of the pan, use a pastry brush dipped in water to brush it away.

Turn up the heat to high and allow to boil rapidly for 5–6 minutes, until the jam thickens and the bubbles start to roll much more slowly.

To test the jam, take your plate from the freezer and put a blob of the jam on it. As it cools, spread it out with your finger. It should be thick and jammy. If it's not, continue to cook for a few minutes until it reaches the right consistency.

Add the butter and stir through. Spoon the jam into your jars and fill to the top. Seal well, and don't forget to label the jars when the jam is cold. Store in the fridge.

Plum jam

Plum jam As plums are rich in pectin, the naturally occurring substance that gives jams their lovely "set" consistency, I use normal sugar rather than jam sugar (sugar with added pectin) here.

Makes 2 x 454g (1lb) jars
Preparation time: 10 minutes
Cooking time: 30 minutes

1kg (2lb 4oz) plums, stones
   removed, cut into eighths
200ml (7fl oz) water
1kg (2lb 4oz) caster sugar
15g (½oz) butter

Place a small plate in the freezer for later and have your jars sterilized, ready to go.

Put the fruit and the 200ml (7fl oz) water into a pan and simmer for 15–20 minutes, or until the fruit is completely soft. Add the sugar to the fruit and stir, still on a low heat, until it has all dissolved. Once the sugar has dissolved, turn up the heat to high and cook for 15–20 minutes.

To test the jam, take your plate from the freezer and put a blob of the jam on it. As it cools, spread it out with your finger. It should be thick and jammy. If it's not, continue to cook for a few minutes until it reaches the right consistency.

Add the small knob of butter and stir through. Spoon the jam into your jars and fill to the top. Seal well, and don't forget to label the jars when the jam is cold. Store in the fridge.

Orange marmalade

Makes 2 x 454g (1lb) jars
Preparation time: 10 minutes
Cooking time: 2 hours

500g (1lb 2oz) oranges
1.5 litres (2¾ pints) water
1kg (2lb 4oz) jam sugar
15g (½oz) butter

Place a small plate in the freezer for later and have your jars sterilized, ready to go.

Squeeze the juice from the oranges into a sieve set over a large pan, scooping out all the pips and pulp. Whatever is left in the sieve, spoon it out into a small piece of muslin cloth and tie with a piece of string. Add this muslin bag to the juice along with the 1.5 litres (2¾ pints) water. Slice the leftover orange shells thinly into strips and add them to the pan.

On a medium heat, bring the contents of the pan to the boil, then reduce the heat and simmer for 1½ hours. After this time the peel should feel soft and be slightly translucent. Carefully remove the muslin bag and allow it to cool. The orange mix can sit off the heat while you're waiting. When cool enough to handle, squeeze the life out of the bag over the mix. This is to extract all the pectin.

Add the sugar to the pan, and cook on a low heat until it has all dissolved. Once dissolved, stop stirring and turn the heat up high so it's boiling rapidly. It will rise up in the pan, but don't worry, this is normal – it will naturally fall back down. After 8–10 minutes (or when it's looking thickened), take your plate from the freezer and put a blob of the marmalade on it. As it cools, spread it out with your finger. It should be thick and jammy. If it's not, continue to cook for a few minutes until it reaches the right consistency.

Add the butter and stir through. Spoon the marmalade into your jars and fill to the top, then seal well and leave to cool. Store in the fridge.

Homemade chocolate & almond spread

At Duck & Waffle, our breakfasts are made special by making things like our own homemade version of Nutella. We use roasted hazelnuts, so the flavour is almost identical to the original, only the consistency is slightly chunkier for that authentic feel. That recipe is in my book *Duck & Waffle, Recipes & Stories*, but for this one I wanted to take it one step further and I've used almonds and almond milk, for a different, more subtle flavour.

This spread is great to have in the fridge: it lasts for a good week, makes a great snack and is a lovely quick-cheat component to a dessert – think a dollop on a cheesecake, or maybe a spoonful mixed into ice cream.

Makes 1 x 454g (1lb) jar
Preparation time: 10 minutes
Cooking time: 15 minutes

50g (1¾oz) chocolate (about 65% cocoa solids, but it's OK to use stronger or weaker)
50g (1¾oz) unsalted almonds
60g (2¼oz) icing sugar
10g (¼oz) cocoa powder
25g (1oz) drinking chocolate powder
75ml (2½fl oz) almond milk

Preheat the oven to 180°C fan/400°F/gas mark 6.

Melt the chocolate in a microwave or in a heatproof bowl set over a pan of barely simmering water.

Put the almonds on a baking tray and roast until golden, approximately 5 minutes. Place in a food processor and blend until ground.

Add the icing sugar, cocoa powder and drinking chocolate and blend together, then add the melted chocolate and blend again. Gradually add the almond milk, still blending, until smooth. Transfer to a sterilized jar and seal. Store in the fridge.

Reuben open top (rye bread, salt beef & Swiss cheese)

The Reuben is a classic. Either from Nebraska or, as is more commonly believed, New York (there are a few theories as to which is true), it's one of the best sandwiches out there – the sandwich that has everything. To me it represents a Saturday lunch with a cold beer, watching the football with friends.

Rather than using the traditional sauerkraut, I prefer the tang of a good gherkin. Let's face it, we all have a jar of gherkins lurking in our cupboard, but few of us have sauerkraut. I also prefer this served as an open sandwich, almost cheese-on-toast style, with the cheese as the crowning glory on top of the meaty goodness.

Makes 2
Preparation time: 10 minutes
Cooking time: 10 minutes

2 slices of rye bread
50g (1¾oz) salt beef/corned beef,
    sliced to your desired thickness
    (I like mine 5mm/¼ inch thick)
2 large gherkins, sliced lengthways,
    5mm (¼ inch) thick
2 slices Swiss cheese
10g (¼oz) butter

Dressing
2 teaspoons mayonnaise
1 tablespoon ketchup
1 teaspoon horseradish sauce
freshly ground black pepper

To make the dressing, mix all the ingredients together and set aside.

Have your grill ready to go, on a medium heat. Take the rye bread and divide the salt beef between the slices, then layer the sliced gherkins on top and finish each one with a slice of cheese.

Heat a non-stick pan over a medium heat and add the butter. When it begins to foam, place each sandwich in the pan and cook it for 1 minute, then put the pan straight under the grill. As the cheese melts, the bottom will start to crisp up.

It'll take about 4 minutes to be ready, by which time the base will be crisp and the cheese will be bubbling. Serve with a good spoon of the dressing on the side.

Smashed avocado with minted goats' cheese (*pictured on page 21*)

This is my go-to breakfast at work – it's quick, tasty and healthy. Avocados are loaded with potassium, and when working the silly hours that us chefs do, it's great to start the day on the right foot. I add a splash of hot sauce too...

Makes 2
Preparation time: 5 minutes
Cooking time: 5 minutes

1 ripe avocado
sea salt flakes and freshly ground
  black pepper
olive oil
2 slices of sourdough bread
50g (1¾oz) semi-hard
  goats' cheese
4 fresh mint leaves, finely sliced
hot sauce, to serve

Halve the avocado, then scoop out the flesh from the skin into a bowl, using a tablespoon. Discard the stone. Using a fork, break down the avocado flesh as much as you like and season with salt and pepper.

Heat a griddle pan over a medium heat. Drizzle some olive oil on a plate and lightly dab each slice of bread in the oil on both sides. Season with salt and pepper. When the pan is hot, char the bread on both sides until nicely browned. Set aside on a plate while you prepare the topping.

Crumble the goats' cheese with your fingers into roughly 5mm (¼ inch) chunks. Add the mint and mix together.

Spread the avocado over both slices of toast and sprinkle (or spoon little blobs on if soft) the minty goats' cheese on top. Finish with a good drizzle of olive oil, a splash of hot sauce and a twist of black pepper. Eat straight away.

Chestnut mushroom, cream cheese & tarragon *(pictured overleaf)*

Mushrooms on toast is a classic, found in pubs and restaurants all over the country. From simple button mushrooms to luxurious morels with Madeira and cream, there's something so comforting about this dish, I never get bored with it. You can use whichever mushrooms you prefer – there is no right or wrong. I use chestnut because I love their subtle nuttiness and they are a little bigger than button.

Serves 2
Preparation time: 5 minutes
Cooking time: 10 minutes

olive oil
100g (3½oz) chestnut mushrooms,
   stems removed, sliced 2–3mm
   (about ⅛ inch) thick
sea salt flakes and freshly ground
   black pepper
10g (¼oz) butter
1 shallot, finely chopped
1 garlic clove, finely chopped
2 tablespoons cream cheese
2 slices of sourdough bread
a pinch of finely chopped
   fresh tarragon

Heat a small frying pan over a medium heat, and add a drizzle of olive oil. When it is hot and almost smoking, add the mushrooms and turn up the heat to high. Allow the mushrooms to colour, and if any juice comes out, let it reduce. After 3–4 minutes the mushrooms will be softened and the juice absorbed back in. Season with salt and pepper.

Add the butter and allow to foam, then add the shallots and garlic and cook for about 3 minutes, until they start to soften. Add the cream cheese and stir through, then turn off the heat and set aside until you're ready to serve.

Heat a griddle pan over a medium heat. Drizzle some olive oil on to a plate and lightly dab each slice of bread in the oil on both sides. Season with salt and pepper. When the pan is hot, char the bread on both sides until nicely browned. Set aside on a plate while you prepare the topping.

Reheat your mushrooms and add the tarragon. Stir through and check the seasoning. Spoon on to the toast and eat immediately.

Ricotta, pear, honey, thyme This is a combination of great ingredients rather than a recipe per se, one that I picked up from my frequent visits to Italy. The Italians have a simple philosophy: "eat great food", always when the ingredients are at their peak. This dish would fall apart if the ricotta used wasn't made with good milk, or if the pears weren't ripe. With simple food there is nowhere to hide. Pears and honey are often served as garnishes for cheese in Italy, so this made sense to me when I imagined putting it all on toast.

Makes 2
Preparation time: 5 minutes
Cooking time: 5 minutes

olive oil
2 slices of sourdough bread
sea salt flakes and freshly ground
   black pepper
1 ripe pear
2 tablespoons ricotta (the best you
   can find)
1 tablespoon honey
1 sprig of fresh thyme, to garnish

Heat a griddle pan over a medium heat.

Drizzle some olive oil over a plate. Lightly dab both sides of each slice of bread in the oil and season with salt and pepper. When the pan is hot, char the bread on both sides until nicely browned. Set aside on a plate while you prepare the topping.

Finely slice the pear. Divide the ricotta between the slices of toast, and top each one with 5–6 slices of pear.

Drizzle with the honey, season with a little pepper and finish with the thyme by pinching the sprig at the base, then stripping the leaves off and sprinkling them all over. Doing this at the last minute releases the fresh aroma of the herb and it tastes fantastic.

Chopped roast beef & mustard This is a great idea for leftovers. If you have roast beef for Sunday lunch, then make this for a tasty Monday snack. You can switch the mustard for horseradish too. If you don't have any leftovers you can either buy cold roast beef from your deli or, alternatively, use salt beef.

Serves 2
Preparation time: 5 minutes
Cooking time: 5 minutes

1 tablespoon English mustard
2 tablespoons mayonnaise
150g (5½oz) leftover roast beef
sea salt flakes and freshly ground
  black pepper
olive oil
2 slices of sourdough bread
a handful of watercress
3 radishes, thinly sliced

To make the chopped beef mix, combine the mustard and mayonnaise. Slice the beef as thick as you like – I'd go for 5mm (⅛ inch) – then run your knife through it the other direction to make strips. Add to the mayo and mix well. Season with salt and pepper.

Heat a griddle pan over a medium heat. Drizzle some olive oil on a plate and lightly dab each slice of bread in the oil on both sides. Season with salt and pepper. When the pan is hot, char the bread on both sides until nicely browned. Set aside on a plate while you prepare the topping.

Lightly dress the watercress and radishes with some olive oil and a pinch of sea salt.

Divide the beef mix between the slices of toast. Scatter the watercress and radish salad on top and eat straight away.

Smoked mackerel, horseradish & pickled beetroot

The combination of mackerel, beetroot and horseradish is a classic for a reason: it tastes amazing. The sweetness/acidity of the pickled beetroot cuts through the earthy richness of the mackerel to make this a lovely dish. Another quick snack that's ideal for a lazy afternoon.

Makes 2
Preparation time: 5 minutes
Cooking time: 5 minutes

2 smoked mackerel fillets
1 tablespoon mayonnaise
2 tablespoons horseradish sauce
olive oil
sea salt flakes and freshly ground
  black pepper
2 slices of sourdough bread
2 pickled beetroots, very thinly
  sliced
finely chopped fresh chives,
  to garnish

Peel the skin off the mackerel and flake the flesh into a bowl with your fingers. Add the mayo and horseradish sauce to the bowl and mix to bind together.

Heat a griddle pan over a medium heat. Drizzle some olive oil on a plate, and lightly dab each slice of bread in the oil on both sides. Season with salt and pepper. When the pan is hot, char the bread on both sides until nicely browned, then place on a serving plate.

Spoon the mackerel-mayo mixture on to the toasts, scatter over the sliced beetroot and finish with a sprinkling of chopped chives.

Oven-roasted tomatoes & goats' cheese

This one is more of a knife and fork job. The juicy tomatoes moisten the bread as you cut into them; kind of like a bruschetta.

Makes 2
Preparation time: 5 minutes
Cooking time: 20 minutes

2 ripe plum tomatoes
olive oil
sea salt flakes and freshly ground
   black pepper
1 sprig of fresh thyme, leaves
   picked
50g (1¾oz) semi-hard goats'
   cheese
2 slices of sourdough bread
a few fresh basil leaves, to garnish

Preheat your oven to 180°C fan/400°F/gas mark 6.

Remove the eye of each tomato and slice in half lengthways. Place each tomato half on a baking tray, cut side up, and drizzle with olive oil. Season with salt and pepper and sprinkle over the thyme leaves. Bake for approximately 15 minutes, until nicely roasted and browned slightly. The tomatoes should be slightly softened.

Take the tomatoes out of the oven and crumble the goats' cheese over each one, then pop back in for a further 5 minutes until the cheese softens and starts to brown. Remove from the oven and leave on the side while you prepare the toast.

Heat a griddle pan over a medium heat. Drizzle some olive oil on a plate, and lightly dab each slice of bread in the oil on both sides. Season with salt and pepper. When the pan is hot, char the bread on both sides until nicely browned, then transfer to a plate.

Top the toast with the roasted tomatoes, 2 halves per slice. Drizzle with olive oil and season with a twist of black pepper. If you have any basil knocking about, tear some on top at the last minute.

Indian-spiced baked beans

This is a mildly spiced take on the British classic beans on toast. I cooked with Cyrus Todiwala when I appeared on *Saturday Kitchen*, and his version of this really impressed me and got me thinking…

Serves 4
Preparation time: 10 minutes
Cooking time: 25 minutes

1 teaspoon cumin seeds
1 tablespoon curry powder
olive oil
1 red onion, finely chopped
2 garlic cloves, finely chopped
1 red chilli, finely chopped, seeds
   left in
sea salt flakes and freshly ground
   black pepper
2 x 400g (14oz) cans of cooked
   white beans, drained
300ml (½ pint) chicken stock
8 slices of sourdough bread
a handful of fresh coriander,
   stalks included, roughly chopped
10g (¼oz) butter

Put the cumin seeds and curry powder in a dry frying pan over a medium heat and toast for a few minutes, shaking the pan, until you can smell the aromas and the spices look toasted. Add a drizzle of olive oil to the pan, then add the onions, garlic and chilli, season with salt and pepper, and cook for 8–10 minutes or until the onions are soft (but don't let them become coloured).

Add the beans and the chicken stock and bring to the boil. Season with salt and pepper. Simmer for 10 minutes – you want the stock to reduce to a stew-like consistency.

Heat a griddle pan over a medium heat. Drizzle some olive oil on a plate and lightly dab each slice of bread in the oil on both sides. Season with salt and pepper. When the pan is hot, char the bread on both sides until nicely browned. Set aside on a plate while you prepare the garnish.

Stir the chopped coriander leaves and stalks into the beans and add the butter. Serve the pot of beans on the table with the toast on the side, or go ahead and spoon them straight on to the toast.

Egg mayonnaise with spring onions, mustard & chives

Egg mayo is a funny one for me – I never thought to make it, but if I saw someone making it or if I found a tub in the fridge, I couldn't help but devour it. I've since got over my denial and have accepted that I'm a huge fan – now I make it regularly at home. It's a great bite when I get back from work late at night. I also like to add some crushed salt and vinegar crisps on top…

Serves 2
Preparation time: 5 minutes
Cooking time: 10 minutes

2 eggs
1 tablespoon mayonnaise
1 teaspoon Dijon mustard
a pinch of finely chopped
   fresh chives, plus extra to garnish
1 spring onion, finely sliced, plus
   extra to garnish
sea salt flakes and freshly ground
   black pepper
olive oil
2 slices of sourdough bread
handful of salt and vinegar crisps
   (optional)

Bring a medium pan of water to the boil and add a pinch of salt. Add the eggs and simmer for 6 minutes. Remove them from the pan and put them straight into iced water to chill as quickly as possible. Peel the eggs, quarter them, then pop them into a mixing bowl. The yolks should be slightly soft.

Add the mayo, mustard, chives and spring onion and season with salt and pepper. Mix together – if the eggs break a little, that's fine.

Heat a griddle pan over a medium heat. Drizzle some olive oil on a plate, and lightly dab each slice of bread in the oil on both sides. Season with salt and pepper. When the pan is hot, char the bread on both sides until nicely browned. Set aside on a plate.

Spoon the egg mix over the toast and finish with a good twist of black pepper and extra chopped chives and spring onion. If you want to try my crisp tip, just take a handful of crisps, hold them over the plate of egg mayo on toast and crush them, letting them fall on top of the egg.

EGGS

2

Eggs are something that I couldn't live without. I have eggs for breakfast every day without fail. Not only are there different ways of cooking them, there are endless garnishes for them too. Add that to the fact that eggs are great at any time and that, let's face it, everything tastes better with an egg on it, and you have the ultimate all-day ingredient.

It's important to use good eggs. If you have a farm shop or a farmers' market nearby, try there. The difference is phenomenal. I really don't think the standard battery chickens' eggs are good for anyone, especially the poor chickens. As cheap as they are, we all need to be a little more aware of what we are doing to animals and putting into our bodies. At the restaurant we only use organic eggs, but free-range are good too.

You may know the basics of poaching, frying, scrambling, etc., but here are a few tips that will maybe make that poached egg rounder or your scrambled eggs lighter...

Poached – Crack each egg into a small ramekin first, rather than straight into the water. Lower the ramekin into the water so it fills up, then, after 20 seconds (or when your fingers can't take the heat anymore) tip the egg out into the water. Doing it this way tempers the egg so it sets quickly and, most importantly, the fall is shorter, so it is less likely for the yolk to pop out or hit the bottom of the pan with impact, breaking the yolk.

Scrambled – I like my scrambled eggs creamy and relatively smooth. Not ultra-smooth (that's why I don't use a whisk when cooking them), but pretty smooth. The trick is to whisk them well in a bowl first, then cook them very slowly over a low heat, in butter, stirring all the time with a wooden spoon. Of course cream helps, a drop at the end, but that's naughty...

Fried – This is a tricky one at the restaurant. To me, a fried egg is slightly crisp on the bottom, but with a runny yolk on top. I've served them that way and they've come straight back to the kitchen, as the guest was after a soft bottom, no colour at all. There is no right or wrong, but understanding how to do both ways is useful. Basically, for a soft bottom, use a little more oil, and cook on a lower heat, much slower, from cold. For a crispy bottom, heat a pan with oil until it's hot, then drop your egg in and cook it quicker. Simples.

Boiled – Always put your eggs into boiling water, and start the timer straight away. You will get inconsistent results if you start your eggs in a pan of cold water and bring to the boil, as the cooking time will depend on how big the pot is, how much water there is and how many eggs you are cooking. For medium eggs from the fridge, I drop them into boiling water for:

    Soft-boiled – 5 minutes
    In the middle – 6 minutes
    Hard-boiled – 8 minutes

"Eggs Benedict" salt beef bagel & mustard hollandaise

Eggs Benedict, along with its siblings Eggs Royal and Eggs Florentine, is up there with the most famous of egg dishes. Traditionally, it's a toasted muffin, sliced ham, a poached egg and a good lashing of hollandaise. In the old days, ox tongue was used instead of ham – someone once told me that the reason ham or tongue was used was to stop the egg from making the muffin go soggy. I really hope that was true. Here, I merge the world of the salt beef bagel with that of the Benedict for a brunch favourite of mine.

Serves 2 (but makes extra hollandaise, as making a smaller portion can be tricky)
Preparation time: 5 minutes
Cooking time: 20 minutes

2 tablespoons white wine vinegar
4 eggs
100g (3½oz) salt beef
1 bagel, halved
butter
1 gherkin, thinly sliced
3 generous tablespoons of
    hollandaise (see below)
freshly ground black pepper

Hollandaise
250g (9oz) butter, clarified
    (see method)
30ml (1fl oz) white wine
30ml (1fl oz) white wine vinegar
2 peppercorns
1 sprig of fresh thyme
2 egg yolks
1 tablespoon wholegrain mustard
sea salt flakes
1 small squeeze of lemon juice

To make the clarified butter for the hollandaise, heat the butter in a small pan over a low heat until the fats and milks separate. Carefully pour off the clear melted butter, leaving the milk sediment in the pan. Discard the sediment.

To make the hollandaise, put the wine, vinegar, peppercorns and thyme into a small pan. Bring to the boil, then simmer until reduced by half. Strain into a mixing bowl. Add the egg yolks and whisk over a bain-marie (a heatproof bowl set over a pan of barely simmering water) until light and fluffy. This should take around 5 minutes. If the water in the pan below the bowl starts to boil, turn off the heat, as there will still be enough heat in the pan to cook the eggs – just be careful they don't scramble.

Slowly start adding the clarified butter until the mixture has a mayonnaise-like consistency. If it gets too thick, add 1 teaspoon of warm water and that will bring it back to life. Stir in the mustard, season with salt and add the lemon juice. The hollandaise will hold in a warm place for at least 30 minutes. Just be careful it's not too warm or it may split – next to your stove should be fine.

Now turn on your grill and bring a pan of water to the boil. Add the white wine vinegar, then, following the poaching tips on page 37, gently poach your eggs. After 3 minutes, they should be firm on the outside yet still soft in the middle. While the eggs are poaching, warm your salt beef under the hot grill for 1–2 minutes, taking care not to let it dry out.

Remove the poached eggs from the pan and put them on a plate lined with kitchen paper to drain. Toast your bagels, then butter them.

To assemble the eggs Benedict, divide the warmed salt beef between the buttered bagel halves, add a few gherkin slices, then put 2 poached eggs on each (if your eggs have lost their heat, just dunk them back in the hot water for 30 seconds, drain on the kitchen paper again, then put them straight on to the salt beef).

Spoon over the hollandaise to cover the eggs, season with pepper and you're good to go.

Poached eggs, grilled broccoli, walnut, brown anchovies & Parmesan

(*pictured on page 43*) Tasty and very healthy – this is my go-to post-gym breakfast. I never feel like eating right after I wake up, but post-gym I'm ravenous and usually for something healthy to set the tone for the day.

Serves 2
Preparation time: 10 minutes
Cooking time: 10 minutes

100g (3½oz) purple sprouting broccoli or a head of regular broccoli cut into smaller florets
50ml (2fl oz) olive oil
4 brown anchovy fillets
2 tablespoons buttermilk
50g (1¾oz) Parmesan cheese, finely grated, plus extra to serve
a small squeeze of lemon juice
2 tablespoons white wine vinegar
4 eggs
4–5 toasted walnuts

Blanch the broccoli in a pan of salted boiling water for about 1 minute, until it's cooked but still has a bite. Refresh in ice-cold water, then drain and pat dry.

Heat a griddle pan over a medium heat. Toss the broccoli in the olive oil, then put it on the griddle and cook until it's nice and browned. This should take 3–5 minutes. When it's cooked, transfer to a plate and set aside.

While the broccoli is cooking, make the anchovy dressing. Finely chop the anchovy fillets. Pop them into a small bowl, then add the buttermilk and Parmesan and stir well. Add the lemon juice and stir in.

To poach the eggs, bring a pan of water to the boil and add the white wine vinegar. Following the poaching tips on page 37, gently poach your eggs. After 3 minutes, they should be firm on the outside yet soft in the middle. Remove them from the pan and put them on a plate lined with kitchen paper to drain.

Put the broccoli and anchovy dressing into a mixing bowl and toss together until nicely coated. Divide between 2 plates and pop 2 poached eggs on each plate. Grate a little extra Parmesan over and finish by crushing the walnuts on top. Eat straight away.

Devilled eggs (*pictured overleaf*) I'm addicted to these. They are quick and easy to make, with ingredients I generally have in my fridge at home, which means I have them way more often than I probably should. Try using them as part of a platter when you have friends round to watch the football or for a movie night. Make sure you have plenty though!

Makes enough for 4
Preparation time: 5 minutes
Cooking time: 10 minutes

8 eggs, hard-boiled and shelled
1 tablespoon mayonnaise
1 teaspoon Sriracha (or any hot sauce you have)
1 sprig of fresh coriander, finely chopped
1 shallot, finely chopped

Garnish
fresh coriander leaves
1 green chilli, sliced finely on the angle
2 spring onions, finely sliced
1 tablespoon toasted sesame seeds

Halve your hard-boiled eggs vertically and slide out the yolks without breaking the whites. Set aside the egg whites. Put the yolks into a blender, and add the mayo and Sriracha. Blend until smooth, then transfer to a bowl. Add the chopped coriander and shallot and stir through.

Spoon the mixture into the cavity of each reserved half egg white, and put the filled eggs on to a plate. Garnish with the coriander leaves, sliced chilli and spring onions and sprinkle the sesame seeds on top to finish.

Baked eggs, potatoes, roasted peppers, onions & goats' cheese

Baking eggs like this is one of my favourite ways of using up leftovers. Take whatever is knocking about in your fridge that may work well together, heat it up for a bit in the oven, then crack an egg or two on top, pop it back in the oven to cook the eggs, et voilà! This particular combination is a regular in my house, but you can mix it up how you like.

Serves 2–4
Preparation time: 5 minutes
Cooking time: 20 minutes

olive oil
1 handful of cooked new potatoes,
    sliced 5mm (¼ inch) thick
sea salt flakes and freshly ground
    black pepper
½ red onion, finely sliced
2 tablespoons roasted red peppers
    (from a jar or packet is fine),
    sliced
4 eggs
50g (1¾oz) goats' cheese, crumbled
chopped parsley, to garnish

Preheat the oven to 180°C fan/400°F/gas mark 6.

Take a large metal skillet or an ovenproof non-stick pan, add a drizzle of oil, scatter the potatoes evenly over the base and season with salt and pepper. Heat the pan on the stovetop over a medium heat until the potatoes are sizzling nicely, then add the onions, give the mixture a stir and pop the pan into the oven for 5 minutes. Give the pan a good shake, then put it back into the oven for a further 5 minutes, or until the potatoes are golden.

Add the roasted peppers to the pan and crack the eggs on top. Bake in the oven for 5 minutes, or until the egg whites start to set. Crumble over the goats' cheese and add another drizzle of olive oil.

Bake for a final 2–3 minutes, depending on how soft you like your eggs. Season with salt and pepper and finish with a sprinkle of chopped parsley.

Coddled eggs with spinach & mushrooms, Marmite soldiers

Coddled eggs are cooked slowly in special little pots within a bain marie until soft and creamy. Not many people have the pots at home, myself included, so I use ramekins instead. I love how the egg breaks into the sauce for a truly luscious dish. As Marmite can be controversial, it is, of course, optional…

Serves 4
Preparation time: 20 minutes
Cooking time: 10 minutes

50g (1¾oz) butter
100g (3½oz) chestnut mushrooms
  (button are fine too), quartered
sea salt flakes and freshly ground
  black pepper
100g (3½oz) spinach leaves,
  washed
4 eggs
8 tablespoons double cream
4 slices of bread
Marmite

Preheat the oven to 180°C fan/400°F/gas mark 6. Using 10g (¼oz) of the butter, grease 4 ramekins.

Heat a saucepan over a medium heat, and add 20g (¾oz) of the butter. Add the mushrooms and sauté them, seasoning at the end so the juice doesn't come out and make them stew. Remove the mushrooms to a plate, then add the remaining butter to the pan. Add the spinach and cook until wilted, then season with salt and pepper.

Divide the spinach between the prepared ramekins, and put the mushrooms on top. Crack an egg into each ramekin, then top each with 2 tablespoons of double cream. Finish with a pinch of salt and a twist of black pepper. Put the ramekins in a roasting dish, then pour boiling water into the dish to come halfway up the sides of the ramekins. Bake for 6–8 minutes or until the eggs are set, but are still nice and soft.

While the eggs are baking, toast the bread and spread it with Marmite. Cut it into soldiers so you're all ready to go. Serve the eggs straight from the oven with the Marmite soldiers.

Turkish eggs, yoghurt, chorizo butter, mint

I fell in love with this dish having first eaten it at Kopapa in Covent Garden. It was such a surprise to me, I couldn't imagine it working at all but, when I ate that first bite, it all made sense. That was the dish that inspired me to make this version. I use chorizo to infuse the butter and leave the meat in for a bit of texture. I recommend you serve it with toast, and lots of it, to mop up all those juices.

Serves 2
Preparation time: 15 minutes
Cooking time: 5 minutes

1 x 80g (2¾oz) chorizo sausage, skin removed, diced
50g (1¾oz) butter
100g (3½oz) Greek yoghurt
2 tablespoons white wine vinegar
4 eggs
4–5 fresh mint leaves, finely sliced, to garnish
sea salt flakes and freshly ground black pepper

In a frying pan, lightly sauté the chorizo for a few minutes over a medium heat until it releases its natural oil. Add the butter and allow to melt and bubble together for 2–3 minutes, then turn off the heat and set aside.

Put the yoghurt into a pan and gently warm through. Don't boil, or it'll curdle and split. You want it to be warm, not hot.

To poach the eggs, bring a pan of water to the boil and add the white wine vinegar. Following the poaching tips on page 37, gently poach your eggs. After 3 minutes, they should be firm on the outside yet soft in the middle. Remove them from the pan and put them on a plate lined with kitchen paper to drain.

Now is the time to toast your bread.

Divide the warm yoghurt between 2 bowls and spoon the eggs on top. Using a spoon, lift the chorizo out of the frying pan and scatter it around each bowl, then divide all the butter from the pan between them. It looks like a lot of fat, but trust me – this is what it's all about. Sprinkle over the mint, and season with salt and pepper. Break into the eggs and allow all the components to just fall into one another.

Harissa bolognese baked eggs, runny cheese

This dish combines three of my favourite things. A slow-cooked ragoût, eggs and cheese. I think it's totally justifiable to make a ragoût especially for this recipe, but then I am a glutton. Why not make a hearty pasta dish one night, making a little extra ragoût, and treat yourself to a quick and tasty brunch the next day?

Serves 4
Preparation time: 5 minutes
Cooking time: 2½ hours if making the ragoût, 15 minutes if not

2 tablespoons white wine vinegar
8 eggs
120g (4¼oz) Gruyère cheese, grated

Ragoût
olive oil
500g (1lb 2oz) minced beef
1 onion, finely diced
1 celery stick, finely diced
1 carrot, finely diced
2 garlic cloves, crushed
1 sprig of fresh thyme
1 sprig of fresh rosemary
2 tablespoons harissa
  (see page 171)
1 large glass of red wine
250ml (9fl oz) passata
250ml (9fl oz) beef stock
sea salt flakes and freshly ground
  black pepper

To make the ragoût, heat a small casserole over a medium heat and add a splash of olive oil. Add the minced beef and allow it to brown, using a wooden spoon to break it down into smaller pieces. As the fat starts to come out of the meat, pour it off so the pan stays relatively dry. When all the meat is seared and the fat is gone, after about 10 minutes, add another slug of olive oil, then add the onion, celery, carrot, garlic, thyme, rosemary and harissa.

Cook for a further 10 minutes, or until the veg are soft and become a little coloured. Add the wine and reduce by three-quarters, then add the passata and beef stock and turn down the heat to low. Simmer for approximately 2 hours, then season with salt and pepper and set aside. You will need 200g (7oz) of ragoût for this dish.

When ready to serve, preheat the oven to 180°C fan/400°F/gas mark 6, and reheat your ragoût if using yesterday's leftovers.

To poach the eggs, bring a pan of water to the boil, add the white wine vinegar, then, following the poaching tips on page 37, gently poach your eggs. After 3 minutes, they should be firm on the outside yet soft in the middle. Remove them from the pan and put them on a plate lined with kitchen paper to drain.

Pour the hot ragoût into an earthenware dish, so it's about 2cm (¾ inch) deep. Place the poached eggs on the ragoût, evenly spaced out. Scatter the grated cheese all over and bake for 5 minutes, or until the cheese has melted, then serve.

Eggy bread bacon & cheese sarnie Eggy bread is something my mum used to make me as a kid when I was sick, so for me it conjures up memories of days off school watching kids' TV. The power some food has to transport us back to our childhood never ceases to amaze me. Here, I've added bacon and cheese because, well, why not…

Serves 2
Preparation time: 10 minutes
Cooking time: 10 minutes

6 rashers of bacon
4 eggs
sea salt flakes and freshly ground
  black pepper
4 slices of white bread
25g (1oz) butter
60g (2¼oz) grated Cheddar cheese

Preheat your grill to a medium heat, then grill the bacon until crisp.

Meanwhile, beat the eggs in a wide bowl and season with salt and pepper. Dunk the bread slices into the beaten egg one by one, pressing well so that the bread absorbs as much of the egg as possible, then lay them out on a baking tray. Divide the cooked bacon between 2 of the slices, sprinkle them with half the cheese, then put the remaining slices of bread on top to make 2 sandwiches.

Heat a frying pan over a medium heat and add the butter. When it begins to foam, add the sandwiches. (If your pan is too small, you can do them one by one, using half the butter each time.) After 2 minutes or so, they should be nicely sealed and golden brown. Turn them over and cook the other side.

Sprinkle the rest of the cheese on top, then put the pan under the grill for 2–3 minutes until the cheese melts.

Mexican eggs Following on from the success of the Colombian eggs at the restaurant, this is 'Mark II'. I love a bit of spice in the morning and if that involves avocado then it's happy days.

Makes 2
Preparation time: 10 minutes
Cooking time: 5 minutes

4 slices of sourdough bread
olive oil
50g (1¾oz) butter
4 eggs
50g (1¾oz) Cheddar cheese,
  grated

Salsa
½ avocado
1 plum tomato
¼ red onion, finely chopped
1 teaspoon chipotle paste
50ml (2fl oz) olive oil, plus extra
  for frying the eggs
1 lime, zest and juice
sea salt flakes and freshly ground
  black pepper
2 sprigs of fresh coriander,
  finely chopped

First, make the salsa. Peel the avocado and cut it into 1cm (½ inch) squares. Deseed the tomato and chop it the same way. Mix in a bowl with the red onion, chipotle paste, olive oil and lime zest and juice and season with salt and pepper. Finally, add the coriander and set aside.

Toast the bread and place it on serving plates. Next, fry your eggs. Put a frying pan over a medium heat, then add a splash of oil and the butter. When the butter begins to foam, crack in your eggs and gently fry until the whites are set. Spoon the butter over the yolks during cooking to warm them through, but not too much, unless you want your eggs hard.

Serve the eggs on top of the toast. Spoon the salsa on top of the eggs, season with salt and pepper and finish with the grated cheese.

Egg, spinach & feta tarts with honey & poppy seeds

I love filo tarts – they are incredibly moreish. The crisp flaky pastry is a great vehicle for so many ingredients. This is the kind of dish I use for brunch parties where you have a plethora of dishes to get stuck into.

Makes 4
Preparation time: 10 minutes
Cooking time: 10 minutes

30g (1oz) butter
100g (3½oz) spinach leaves
sea salt flakes and freshly ground
   black pepper
4 x A4 size sheets of filo pastry
4 eggs
100g (3½oz) feta cheese
4 tablespoons honey
1 tablespoon poppy seeds

Preheat your oven to 160°C fan/350°F/gas mark 4.

Heat a saucepan over a medium heat and add 10g (¼oz) of the butter. Add the spinach and cook until wilted. Season with salt and pepper, then drain well in a colander.

Melt the remaining butter in a small pan over a low heat, then, using a pastry brush, brush it around the insides of 4 ramekins.

For each tart, use 1 sheet of filo. Open up the sheet, brush it with some of the butter, then fold it in half and brush with butter one more time. Lay the sheets in the ramekins, scrunching up the sides a bit. Divide the spinach evenly between the ramekins, then crack an egg on top of each. Crumble the feta over each egg.

Bake for 8 minutes, or until the pastry is crisp and golden and the eggs are set but still soft inside.

Drizzle each tart with 1 tablespoon of the honey and sprinkle with a pinch of poppy seeds.

Smoked salmon & cream cheese Scotch eggs

I adore Scotch eggs and have served them in many different forms, including the Scotch Bhaji on page 120. You can't beat a runny egg encased within a crisp coating. This is a nice brunch-style version; prepped in advance, it's an easy win at brunch parties, or a fun addition to a picnic basket.

Makes 4
Preparation time: 20 minutes
Cooking time: 10 minutes

4 eggs
oil, for deep-frying
sea salt flakes

Salmon mousse
200g (7oz) smoked salmon
1 egg white
50g (1¾oz) cream cheese
30ml (1fl oz) double cream

Coating
50g (1¾oz) flour
1 egg, beaten
50g (1¾oz) breadcrumbs

Sauce
2 tablespoons mayonnaise
1 teaspoon horseradish sauce
a few stalks of fresh chives,
    finely chopped

Salad
100g (3½oz) watercress
2 tablespoons olive oil
sea salt flakes

Cook the eggs in a pan of salted boiling water for 5 minutes. Transfer to a bowl of ice-cold water and allow to cool for 10 minutes, then carefully remove the shells and set aside.

To make the mousse, roughly chop half the smoked salmon. Put the other half into a blender. Blend until smooth, then add the egg white and blend again for 20 seconds. Spoon into a mixing bowl and stir in first the cream cheese, then the cream. Lastly, stir in the chopped salmon.

Lay a sheet of clingfilm on your work surface. Add a tablespoon of the salmon mix and spread it out to 1.5cm (⅝ inch) thick. Pop a shelled egg on top, then take another spoon of salmon mix and work it over until it meets the other side. Pick up the clingfilm and use it to shape an even-sized ball. Repeat with the other 3 eggs and put them on a plate.

Preheat the oil a deep-fat fryer to 160°C/325°F.

Now we need to breadcrumb the eggs. Put the flour in one shallow bowl, the breadcrumbs in another and the egg in another. Unwrap the Scotch eggs and lightly coat each one in the flour, tapping off the excess. Next dip them into the egg, and then into the breadcrumbs. Lower them into the deep-fat fryer and cook for 7 minutes.

Meanwhile, make the sauce. Mix together the mayo and horseradish sauce, then add the chives. Dress the watercress with the olive oil and season with salt.

Serve the eggs, cut in half – the yolk should be nice and runny – with the salad and a good spoonful of the sauce alongside.

Cauliflower curry, boiled eggs & coconut crumble

I fell in love with vegetable curries while spending time in India and Bangladesh – cauliflower curry being one of my favourites. The coconut works really well, adding flavour and a rich creaminess, with a crunch in the topping.

Serves 4–6
Preparation time: 10 minutes
Cooking time: 30 minutes

olive oil
1 cauliflower, broken into florets
1 tablespoon cumin seeds
1 tablespoon coriander seeds
1 teaspoon ground turmeric
1 teaspoon onion seeds
1 tablespoon curry powder
1 onion, finely chopped
2.5cm (1 inch) piece of ginger, grated
4 garlic cloves, crushed
1 red chilli, finely chopped
150g (5½oz) cooked yellow lentils
2 x 400ml (14fl oz) cans of coconut milk
sea salt flakes and freshly ground black pepper
2 tablespoons desiccated coconut
8 eggs, hard-boiled and shelled
a large sprig of coriander

Heat some olive oil in a frying pan over a medium heat and brown the cauliflower florets on all sides.

Meanwhile put the cumin seeds, coriander seeds, ground turmeric, onion seeds and curry powder in a dry frying pan over a medium heat and toast for a few minutes, shaking the pan, until you can smell the aromas and the spices look toasted.

Add the onion to the cauliflower pan and cook over a medium heat without letting it colour for 5–6 minutes, or until soft. Add the ginger, garlic and red chilli and cook for a further 3 minutes, again without letting them colour. Stir in the toasted spices and cook for 3 minutes, then add the cooked lentils and pour over the coconut milk. Season with salt and pepper, then reduce the heat and simmer for 10 minutes.

Meanwhile, in a dry pan, toast the desiccated coconut over a medium heat, shaking the pan, until golden brown.

After the final 10 minutes cooking time, the cauliflower should be cooked but retain a little bite. Add the eggs and cook for 3–5 minutes more. Roughly chop the coriander, stalks included, and stir through.

Transfer to a serving dish and scatter the toasted coconut all over, like a crumble, then serve.

HASH, EGGS
OVER EASY

Hash, from the French word *hacher* meaning "to chop", is where the whole idea for this book came from. The classic bubble and squeak sets the bar pretty high. Hash is essentially meat and potatoes, plus anything else you have lying around, chopped together and slowly sautéd or fried, and it's the ultimate all-day, comfort, hangover, hug-on-a-plate frugal feast. There is no better way to use leftovers in my opinion, especially when they're from a roast.

You'll find lots of similarities between the ingredients and methods in the following recipes: potatoes, onion in some form and, as always, butter. However, the single, non-negotiable component in my house is eggs. Fried eggs, over easy. They are the crowning glory. The runny yolk is the missing piece of the puzzle; it's what brings everything together. Why over easy? Too many times I've had runny fried eggs and the yolk has been cold. Here are a few tips to achieve the perfect hash...

Eggs, over easy – Following the cooking guide on page 37, fry your eggs as normal, then, just before serving, carefully turn them over and leave for 30 seconds off the heat. Then turn them back over and serve. Runny, but hot. Dreamland. As you cut into the egg and the yolk runs down the crunchy potato, over the crisp meat and through the sautéed onions, you'll know what I mean.

Potatoes – Leftover roasties make the best hash base – that's a fact. As a general rule when cooking hash, if the potatoes break up a little, that's fine, as these are the bits that will go crisp. If your potatoes are a firmer, use a potato masher once all the ingredients are in the pan, to crush them a little.

Everything else – Broccoli is a winner in a hash, as is cabbage. Any chopped roast meat works, as do sausage and bacon. Veggies on their own are fine too, and curried is a dream. When the hash is in full swing, the ingredients will start to fall into one another, soften up and stick to the pan a little, which is fine – this is the good stuff. Be sure to scrape it all off the pan when serving. If the hash gets a little dry, add a splash of olive oil or another knob of butter.

Black pudding & yesterday's potatoes

This dish is rich and earthy, and feels wonderfully gluttonous – perfect for a tender Sunday morning.

Serves 2
Preparation time: 5 minutes
Cooking time: 20 minutes

a handful of leftover roasties
   (or 1 large potato, cooked
   and peeled)
100g (3½oz) black pudding
25g (1oz) butter
sea salt flakes and freshly ground
   black pepper
2 spring onions, finely sliced
2 eggs
brown sauce, to serve

Cut the potatoes and the black pudding into 2cm (¾ inch) cubes, or thereabouts.

Melt half the butter in a frying pan over a medium heat and sauté the potatoes for about 6–8 minutes, or until they start to brown. Season with salt and pepper.

Add the spring onions to the pan and continue to sauté for 3–4 minutes – if they become a little coloured, this is fine.

Stir in the black pudding and allow everything to cook slowly for 4–5 minutes over a low heat, tossing every 2 minutes or so. Season with more salt and pepper.

Towards the end of the cooking time, melt the remaining butter in another frying pan and fry the eggs.

Divide the hash between 2 plates, top with a fried egg each, and have lashings of brown sauce, or the sauce of your choice, at the ready.

Curried cauliflower & Brussels sprouts

(*pictured on page 70*) Cauliflower works great with Indian spices, I even have another recipe using Indian-spiced cauliflower in this book (see page 60). The spices combined with the vegetables remind me of the style of breakfasts I had when I was in India – they blew me away and inspired dishes like this.

Serves 2
Preparation time: 10 minutes
Cooking time: 30 minutes

½ cauliflower, cut into florets
10–15 Brussels sprouts
25g (1oz) butter
a handful of leftover roasties
    (or 1 large potato, cooked
    and peeled)
1 teaspoon cumin seeds
1 teaspoon curry powder
1 shallot, finely sliced
sea salt flakes and freshly ground
    black pepper
2 eggs
a few sprigs of fresh coriander

Blanch the cauliflower and the Brussels sprouts in boiling water for 2 minutes, then drain. Refresh the Brussels sprouts in cold water and cut them in half.

Cut the potatoes into 2cm (¾ inch) cubes, or thereabouts. Melt half the butter in a frying pan over a medium heat, add the potatoes, cauliflower, cumin seeds and curry powder and sauté for about 6–8 minutes. If they become a little coloured, this is fine.

Add the Brussels sprouts and sliced shallot to the potato mix and allow everything to cook together slowly over a low heat, tossing every 2 minutes or so, for 5–6 minutes. Season with salt and pepper.

Towards the end of the cooking time, melt the remaining butter in another frying pan and fry the eggs.

Roughly chop the coriander, stalks included, and stir into the mix. Divide the hash between 2 plates, and top each one with an egg.

Buttery parsnip & apple, grilled bacon chop (*pictured overleaf*)

A classic, with all the flavours of a good old hog roast. The recipe calls for chops, but leftover roast pork works a treat too.

Serves 2
Preparation time: 10 minutes
Cooking time: 30 minutes

a handful of leftover roasties (or 1
  large potato, cooked and peeled)
25g (1oz) butter
1 shallot, finely sliced
1 parsnip, peeled and grated
1 apple, peeled, cored and cut into
  1cm (½ inch) dice
sea salt flakes and freshly ground
  black pepper
olive oil
2 bacon chops
2 eggs
5–6 leaves of fresh sage, chopped

Cut the potatoes into 2cm (¾ inch) cubes, or thereabouts. Melt half the butter in a frying pan on a medium heat and sauté the potatoes for about 6–8 minutes, or until they start to brown. Add the onions and continue to sauté for 3–4 minutes – if they become a little coloured, this is fine.

Add the grated parsnip and the apples to the pan and allow everything to cook slowly together over a low heat, tossing every 2 minutes or so, for 10–12 minutes. Season with salt and pepper.

Meanwhile, heat a griddle pan over a medium heat. Lightly rub some olive oil into the bacon chops and season with salt and pepper. Cook the chops on the griddle pan for 3–4 minutes on each side, until cooked and hot through, then rest them on a wire rack.

Melt the remaining butter in another frying pan and fry the eggs.

Finish the hash with the chopped sage, then divide between 2 plates, put a chop on each, and finish off with a fried egg.

Bubble & squeak, smoked ham

There really are no rules for this dish. Anything that makes it into a roast dinner is good in a bubble and squeak the next day. My suggestion is that it's made up of half potato and half "other stuff". That can be meat, vegetables, stuffing and bread sauce; the usual suspects. I've made this recipe based on the typical things I have with my roast, but you can, of course, use whatever leftovers you have. I add some cold smoked ham to mine too, but you don't have to.

Serves 2
Preparation time: 10 minutes
Cooking time: 30 minutes

a handful of leftover roasties
    (or 1 large potato, cooked
    and peeled)
25g (1oz) butter
sea salt flakes and freshly ground
    black pepper
½ onion, finely sliced
3 slices of roast beef, chopped into
    1–2cm (½–¾ inch) pieces
2–3 leftover broccoli florets
a handful of leftover carrots,
    peeled and cut into 1cm
    (½ inch) dice
2 eggs
2 slices of smoked ham
1 tablespoon horseradish sauce,
    to serve

Cut the potatoes into 2cm (¾ inch) cubes, or thereabouts. Melt half the butter in a frying pan on a medium heat and sauté the potatoes for about 6–8 minutes, or until they start to brown. Season with salt and pepper. Add the onions and continue to sauté for 3–4 minutes – if they become a little coloured, this is fine.

Add the beef, broccoli and carrots and allow everything to cook slowly over a low heat, tossing every 2 minutes or so, for 10–12 minutes. Season with more salt and pepper.

Towards the end of the cooking time, melt the remaining butter in another frying pan and fry the eggs.

Divide the hash between 2 plates, add a slice of ham on each, then top with 1 egg per plate and serve with the horseradish sauce on the side.

Corned beef, mustard Corned beef has developed a bit of a bad reputation over the years, being best known as a rationed tinned food during the war. The "corning" element refers to the corns of salt used to cure the meat. When called salt beef, however, the perception dramatically changes...

Serves 2
Preparation time: 10 minutes
Cooking time: 30 minutes

a handful of leftover roasties (or 1
    large potato, cooked and peeled)
25g (1oz) butter
sea salt flakes and freshly ground
    black pepper
½ onion, finely sliced
100g (3½oz) corned beef, cut into
    2cm (¾in) cubes
1 tablespoon grain mustard
2 eggs
2 handfuls of watercress
olive oil

Cut the potatoes into 2cm (¾ inch) cubes, or thereabouts. Melt half the butter in a frying pan over a medium heat and sauté the potatoes for about 5 minutes, or until they start to brown. Season with salt and pepper. Add the onions and continue to sauté for 3–4 minutes – if they become a little coloured, this is fine.

Add the corned beef to the pan, and allow everything to cook slowly over a low heat, tossing every 2 minutes or so, for 10–12 minutes. Season with more salt and pepper, then stir in the grain mustard.

Towards the end of the cooking time, melt the remaining butter in another frying pan and fry the eggs.

Divide the hash between 2 plates, top each plate with a fried egg each and season with salt and pepper. Dress the watercress with olive oil and scatter over the top.

Colcann-bac-on Adding bacon to any hash is an obvious thing to do, so "porking" up this Irish classic had to be done.

Serves 2
Preparation time: 10 minutes
Cooking time: 20 minutes

50g (1¾oz) curly kale, roughly
   chopped
a handful of leftover roasties
   (or 1 large potato, cooked
   and peeled)
6 rashers of bacon, cut into 1cm
   (½ inch) pieces
½ onion, finely sliced
sea salt flakes and freshly ground
   black pepper
2 eggs
15g (½oz) butter

Blanch the kale in boiling water for 1 minute, then drain. Cut the potatoes into 2cm (¾ inch) cubes, or thereabouts. Fry the bacon in a frying pan over a medium heat until the fat is released and the bacon starts to brown. Add the onions and the potatoes and sauté in the bacon fat for about 6–8 minutes, or until they start to colour.

Add the kale to the frying pan, and allow everything to cook slowly over a low heat, tossing every 2 minutes or so, for 10–12 minutes. Season with salt and pepper.

Towards the end of the cooking time, melt the butter in another frying pan and fry the eggs.

Divide the hash between 2 plates and top each with an egg.

Smoked haddock, crispy onions, curry sauce

I use poached eggs for this recipe rather than fried – I think it works better, as there is quite a bit going on flavour-wise and using poached eggs lightens things up a little. The crispy onions give a nice crunch too.

Serves 2
Preparation time: 15 minutes
Cooking time: 40 minutes

2 pieces of smoked haddock,
   approx. 125g (4½oz) each,
   skinned and cut into 2cm
   (¾in) cubes
2 eggs

Curry sauce
olive oil
½ onion, finely diced
2 garlic cloves, crushed
a 2cm (¾ inch) piece of ginger,
   finely diced
1 red chilli, finely diced
½ teaspoon cumin seeds
½ teaspoon coriander seeds
1 teaspoon curry powder
sea salt flakes and freshly ground
   black pepper
200ml (7fl oz) chicken stock
200ml (7fl oz) double cream
juice of ½ lemon
a large sprig of fresh coriander,
   chopped, including stalks

Crispy onions
300ml (½ pint) sunflower oil
1 tablespoon plain flour
1 tablespoon curry powder
½ onion, finely sliced

Hash
a handful of leftover roasties
   (or 1 large potato, cooked
   and peeled)
25g (1oz) butter
½ onion, finely sliced
olive oil

To make the curry sauce, heat the olive oil in a medium pan and add the onions and garlic. Cook over a medium heat for 5–6 minutes, or until the onions are soft. Add the ginger, chilli, cumin, coriander and curry powder and cook for a further 3 minutes. Season with salt and pepper.

Add the chicken stock and cook until reduced by half. Add the cream, lower the heat and simmer for 5 minutes.

For the crispy onions, put the oil into a medium pan and heat to 180°C (350°F). (To test if the oil is at the right temperature, drop a cube of bread into the oil. If it turns golden, it's ready). Mix the flour and curry powder together. Toss the sliced onions in the flour mix, then transfer to a sieve and shake off any excess. When the oil is up to temperature, add the onions, taking care they don't stick together too much. After 2–3 minutes, they should be crisp and golden. Remove them from the oil and place them on a plate lined with kitchen paper to dry. Season with sea salt flakes.

To make the hash, cut the potatoes into 2cm (¾ inch) cubes, or thereabouts. Melt half the butter in a frying pan over a medium heat and sauté the potatoes for about 6–8 minutes, or until they start to brown. Add the onions and continue to sauté for 3–4 minutes – if they become a little coloured, this is fine.

Bring the curry sauce back to the boil and drop in the haddock. Simmer for 6–7 minutes, until the haddock is cooked. It should flake when pressed with a spoon.

Meanwhile, let the hash continue to cook for a further 5–6 minutes until it's nice and crisp. Season it with salt and pepper.

Heat a pan of water and poach your eggs, following the poaching guidelines on page 37.

When the haddock is ready, add the lemon juice and chopped coriander to the curry sauce.

Divide the hash between 2 plates, spoon the fish on to each, with a good spoonful of the curry sauce, and top each plate with a poached egg. Finish with some crispy onions on top.

Chicken, harissa, feta & sweet potato

This is the only hash recipe in which I use sweet potato rather than regular potato. Using sweet potato makes for a softer, sweeter and, in some ways, more summery hash. Imagine roasting them over coals when having a barbecue, then turning them into a hash the next day. The chicken benefits from being marinated the day before.

Serves 2
Preparation time: 10 minutes
Cooking time: 1½ hours

2 chicken legs
3 tablespoons Harissa (see page 171)
sea salt flakes and freshly ground black pepper
1 large sweet potato
olive oil
2 spring onions, finely sliced
small can (about 200g/7oz) of sweetcorn, drained
25g (1oz) butter
2 eggs
zest of 1 lemon
50g (1¾oz) feta cheese

Preheat your oven to 180°C fan/400°F/gas mark 6.

Cut the chicken legs through the middle, separating the thighs and drumsticks. Put them into a bowl, then add 2 tablespoons of the harissa and massage it into the flesh. Season with salt and pepper. Put the chicken into a roasting tray and roast for 45 minutes.

Pierce the sweet potato and wrap it in foil. Put it into the oven alongside the chicken and bake for 45 minutes. When the chicken is cooked, take it out of the oven and leave it to rest on a wire rack. Remove the potato and set it aside to cool.

Heat a splash of olive oil in a frying pan over a medium heat. Add the spring onions and cook for 3–5 minutes until soft, without letting them colour. Add the sweetcorn and the final tablespoon of harissa and cook for a further 2 minutes. Season with salt and pepper.

When the potato is cool enough to handle, peel away the skin and cut into roughly 2½cm (1 inch) pieces. Flake the chicken, including the skin, into similar sized pieces, then add the potato and chicken to the frying pan with the spring onion and sweetcorn. Give a good stir and allow to sauté together for 5 minutes.

Meanwhile, melt the butter in another frying pan and fry the eggs.

When the hash is ready, divide it between 2 plates, crumble over the feta cheese and finish with a grating of lemon zest. Top each plate with an egg, season with salt and pepper, then serve.

Smoked salmon, horseradish, soured cream & chives

This is another dish that could maybe benefit from a poached egg. I can't make up my mind, and I've eaten it with both a fried egg and a poached egg more times than I care to admit.

Makes 2
Preparation time: 10 minutes
Cooking time: 15 minutes

25g (1oz) butter
a handful of leftover roasties
 (or 1 large potato, cooked
 and peeled)
2 spring onions, finely sliced
½ small packet (about 15g/½oz)
 of fresh chives, finely chopped
2 tablespoons soured cream
4 teaspoons horseradish sauce
2 eggs 100g (3½oz) smoked
 salmon, cut into 2cm (¾ inch)
 slices
sea salt flakes and freshly ground
 black pepper

Cut the potatoes into 2cm (¾ inch) cubes, or thereabouts.

Melt half the butter in a frying pan on a medium heat and sauté the potatoes for about 6–8 minutes, or until they start to brown. Add the spring onions and continue to sauté for 3–4 minutes – if they become a little coloured, this is fine.

In the meantime, put the chives into a small serving bowl. Add the soured cream and horseradish sauce and mix together.

Take the frying pan off the heat, add the smoked salmon to the potatoes and stir to warm through, taking care not to let the residual heat cook the salmon too much. Season with salt and pepper (be careful not to add too much salt, as the salmon can be quite salty).

In another frying pan, melt the remaining butter and fry the eggs. Divide the eggs between 2 plates, top with the hash and season with salt and pepper to taste. Serve with the horseradish and chive soured cream on the side.

PANCAKES

4

Pancakes are wonderful little things. As a kid, Pancake Day was up there with Easter chocolate binges on my calendar of treats. The flat crêpe-style with lemon and sugar was the only type I really knew. That was until around my twelfth or thirteenth birthday, when my parents took me out for a meal as a treat. I ordered blueberry pancakes for dessert.

I wasn't expecting what I received but, my god, was I happy. Fluffy, sweet, light pillows studded with fresh blueberries, topped with creamy vanilla ice cream. My little mind was blown.

Then there was my introduction to crispy bacon and fried eggs with pancakes, all drowned in maple syrup. That was it. I was hooked.

Having been around mountains of waffles for the past four years, I'm finding myself craving pancakes like never before. I've always loved them, but we can't really serve them at the restaurant, and I find one always craves what one can't have. Consequently, I'm pretty sick of waffles now.

Over the page is my recipe for American-style fluffy pancakes, and on the subsequent pages you'll find my various serving suggestions and garnishes. I'm not going to lie; it was pretty tough getting it down to ten recipes, which shows just how much I love making them at home.

American-style pancakes This batter keeps for 1–2 days in the fridge.

Makes 4

125g (4½oz) self-raising flour
a pinch of sea salt flakes
2 eggs, separated
120ml (4fl oz) milk
10g (¼oz) butter

Sift the flour and salt into a mixing bowl and make a well in the middle. Add the egg yolks and milk in the centre then, using a whisk, whisk the flour into them until you have a smooth batter.

In a separate bowl, whisk the egg whites until they form soft peaks. Fold them into the egg-and-flour mixture and you're good to go.

Heat a large frying pan over a medium heat. Add half the butter and, when it's foaming, add 2 50ml (2fl oz) ladlefuls of pancake batter (leaving a gap between them) and cook for 2 minutes, or until light brown on the bottom and starting to set on the top.

Flip over the pancakes and cook for a further minute or so, until brown on the undersides. Transfer to a plate and repeat with the remaining butter and batter to cook 2 more pancakes.

Smoked salmon, spring onion & chive pancakes, eggs & avocado A classic combination, this one is a brunch crowd-pleaser. Here I add some salmon and spring onions to the batter before cooking, which adds a different dimension to the dish. Hollandaise would be a great indulgent addition to this.

Serves 2
Preparation time: 20 minutes
Cooking time: 10 minutes

100g (3½oz) sliced smoked salmon
1 batch of American-style Pancake
  batter (see above)
2 spring onions, finely sliced
1 or 2 stalks of fresh chives,
  finely chopped
50ml (2fl oz) white wine vinegar
4 eggs
1 ripe avocado

Cut half the smoked salmon into ½cm (¼ inch) strips and stir them into the pancake batter along with the spring onions and chives.

Now make your pancakes following the method above.

To poach the eggs, bring a pan of water to the boil and add the white wine vinegar. Following the poaching tips on page 37, gently poach your eggs. After 3 minutes they should be firm on the outside yet soft in the middle.

Halve the avocado, lift out the stone and scoop out the flesh using a tablespoon. Slice each half into strips lengthways, approximately 5mm (¼ inch) thick.

To serve, warm your pancakes through in the pan you cooked them in, then place 2 on each plate. Divide the remaining sliced smoked salmon between the plates, top with the avocado (a quarter per pancake) and finish each serving with 2 poached eggs.

Sweetcorn & sweet potato pancakes, grilled chorizo & cream cheese

This recipe offers a great way to use up leftover sweet potatoes from the night before. Rather than roasting them for 45 minutes, you can peel and steam the potatoes instead to make the whole process much quicker, but I find roasting gives a much better flavour.

Serves 4
Preparation time: 10 minutes
Cooking time: 2 hours

1 sweet potato
150g (5½oz) self-raising flour
4 eggs, plus 4 eggs, separated
1 teaspoon jerk seasoning
150ml (¼ pint) milk
100g (3½oz) sweetcorn kernels
a pinch of salt
2 chorizo sausages
3 tablespoons cream cheese
2 tablespoons hot sauce
40g (1½oz) butter

To serve
sea salt flakes and freshly ground
    black pepper
fresh coriander leaves
1 spring onion, finely sliced on
    an angle

Preheat the oven to 180°C fan/400°F/gas mark 6.

Pierce the sweet potato and wrap it in foil. Bake for 45 minutes, or until cooked. When cooked, set aside until it is cool enough to handle, but leave the oven on. Peel the sweet potato, put it into a food processor and blend to a smooth purée, then scrape out into a mixing bowl. If you don't have a food processor, put the potato into a bowl and break it down with a fork.

Add the flour, egg yolks, jerk seasoning and milk to the bowl with the potato and whisk until smooth. Stir in the sweetcorn kernels. In a separate bowl, whisk the egg whites with the salt until stiff, then fold into the pancake batter.

Put the chorizo sausages on a small baking tray and bake for 10–12 minutes. Place on a plate to cool a little, then cut into 5mm (¼ inch) thick slices.

Mix the cream cheese with the hot sauce and set aside.

Cook the pancakes as per the method on page 88, using half the butter. Keep them warm in a low oven.

Next, fry your eggs using the remaining butter.

Serve 2 pancakes per serving with slices of chorizo on top; add an egg to each plate, season with salt and pepper and add a good dollop of chilli cream cheese on each. Sprinkle with some coriander leaves and spring onion and dive straight in.

Chickpea pancakes, yellow lentil & squash dhal

The dhals I came across in India were quite wet, kind of soup-like. This, of course, varied from town to town, but in general that was the case. Here I make the dhal drier, so it doesn't drown the pancakes. I usually add a couple of fried eggs to this dish too, and some cheese wouldn't go amiss either...

Makes 4
Preparation time: 10 minutes
Cooking time: 1 hour

Pancake batter
olive oil
½ red onion, finely sliced
2 garlic cloves, finely chopped
2 green chillies, finely sliced
100g (3½oz) canned chickpeas
150g (5½oz) chickpea flour, sifted
2 eggs, separated
200ml (7fl oz) water
a pinch of sea salt flakes

Dhal
500g (1lb 2oz) butternut squash,
    peeled and deseeded
olive oil
sea salt flakes and freshly ground
    black pepper
1 onion, finely chopped
2 garlic cloves, finely chopped
a 2½cm (1 inch) piece of ginger,
    finely chopped
1 red chilli, finely chopped
1 teaspoon ground coriander
1 teaspoon ground turmeric
1 teaspoon ground cumin
150g (5½oz) canned yellow lentils
1 x 400g (14oz) tin of chopped
    tomatoes
500ml (18 fl oz) chicken stock
a few sprigs of fresh coriander,
    finely chopped, plus extra leaves
    to garnish
2 tablespoons yoghurt

Preheat your oven to 170°C fan/375°F/gas mark 5.

Cut the squash into 2cm (¾ inch) dice, and spread out on a roasting tray. Drizzle over some olive oil and season with salt and pepper. Bake for 25 minutes, or until the squash starts to colour and has softened.

Next, in a medium pan, add a drizzle of olive oil and the onions and garlic. Season with salt and pepper. Sauté for 4–5 minutes, without letting them colour until soft. Add the ginger and chilli and cook for another minute.

Stir in the ground coriander, turmeric and cumin and cook for 2–3 minutes, then add the lentils, chopped tomatoes and chicken stock. Season with salt and pepper, reduce the heat and simmer for 20 minutes. Add the roasted squash and stir it in. Cook for a further 5 minutes, then turn off the heat and leave to stand while you make the pancakes.

Heat the olive oil in a frying pan over a medium heat. Add the onions and garlic and sauté, without letting them colour, for about 3–4 minutes or until soft. Season with salt and pepper. Add the chillies and cook for a further minute, then transfer to a mixing bowl. Add the chickpeas to the bowl and stir through.

Put the chickpea flour into another mixing bowl and make a well in the centre. Add the egg yolks and start whisking together, adding the water a little at a time until it forms a smooth batter. Stir in the onion and chickpea mix.

Whisk the egg whites with the salt until stiff. Fold them into the chickpea mix, then cook the pancakes following the method on page 88.

When ready to serve, reheat the dhal and stir in the chopped coriander. Serve a good spoonful on top of each pancake, top with a spoonful of yoghurt and season with black pepper. Finish with a few extra coriander leaves to garnish.

Bacon jam, runny eggs Bacon jam is a bit of an obsession of mine and there are so many uses for it. It's great with roasted shellfish, with most meat dishes, on flatbreads… the list goes on. The bacon jam recipe below makes more than you need for this recipe but this is a good thing, believe me – it keeps for a good few weeks in a sterilized jar and, as you'll soon discover, goes with pretty much everything.

Serves 2
Preparation time: 25 minutes
Cooking time: 1 hour

50g (1¾oz) butter
2 eggs
4 American-style Pancakes
   (see page 88)
4 tablespoons Bacon Jam
   (see below)

Bacon jam (Makes 900g/2lb)
500g (1lb 2oz) smoked streaky
   bacon, cut into small lardons
2 onions, finely chopped
2 garlic cloves, finely chopped
2 tablespoons chipotle chilli paste
½ teaspoon smoked paprika
3 tablespoons brown sugar
3 tablespoons treacle
75ml (2½fl oz) cider vinegar
2 shots of espresso

To make the bacon jam, sweat the bacon in a frying pan over a low heat to render the fat. As the fat is released, pour it away so you have just the meat left. Keep cooking until the bacon starts to caramelize. The brown bits that stick to the bottom of the pan are all good, so scrape them off but leave them in the pan.

Add the onions and garlic to the pan and fry, without letting them colour, until soft. Add the chipotle chilli paste, smoked paprika and brown sugar and cook for a further 5 minutes.

Pour in the treacle, vinegar and espresso and simmer gently until it reaches a jam-like consistency – this should take an hour or so. If you need to add a splash of water to keep the jam moist, go for it.

Next, fry your eggs. Melt the butter in a frying pan over a medium heat. When it begins to foam, crack in your eggs and gently fry until the whites are set. Spoon the butter over the yolks to warm them through during cooking, but not too much, unless you want your eggs to be hard.

To serve, warm the pancakes and spread over the bacon jam. Serve 2 on each plate, add a fried egg per person and season with salt and pepper.

Honey-roasted pear, walnut and vanilla ice cream

Homemade ice cream is a wonderful thing but I don't think it's always entirely necessary to make your own. It takes a lot of time and freezer space most people simply don't have. I have included a recipe should you wish to give it a go, but don't feel guilty if you buy it – I won't tell if you don't.

Serves 2

Preparation time: 20 minutes, plus cooling and freezing, if making ice cream, 10 minutes if not

Cooking time: 30 minutes if making ice cream, 10 minutes if not

1 pear
50g (1¾oz) walnuts
20g (¾oz) butter
a pinch of ground cinnamon
50ml (2fl oz) runny honey
4 American-style Pancakes (see page 88)

Vanilla ice cream (Makes 1 litre/ 1¾ pints)
500ml (18fl oz) milk
500ml (18fl oz) double cream
1 vanilla pod
190g (6¾oz) caster sugar
10 egg yolks

To make the ice cream, bring the milk, cream and vanilla to the boil in a large pan. Meanwhile, put the sugar and egg yolks into a bowl and whisk very well. Sugar absorbs moisture, so if you don't start mixing them immediately you will have pieces of dried egg yolk where all the moisture has been removed by the sugar, so beware.

Once the milk and cream come to the boil, pour half on to the yolk mix and whisk together. Add this back to the remaining milk and cream in the pan and heat gently until thickened. In the kitchen we use a thermometer to check when it is cooked – 84°C (183°F) is the temperature we take it to (any higher and the egg will scramble, leaving your ice cream lumpy) – but if you don't have one, cook until it coats the back of a wooden spoon and stays there without running off straight away. Sieve the mix and transfer to another bowl to stop it cooking, then leave to cool and churn.

If you don't have an ice cream machine, freeze the mix in 4 batches and, once frozen, blend in a food processor. Return to the freezer after blending.

Cut the pear into quarters and remove the core. Cut each quarter lengthways into slices approximately 5mm (¼ inch) thick. Set aside.

Heat a small frying pan and add the walnuts. Toast gently over a low heat, taking care not to let them colour too much. Transfer to a plate and leave to cool. When cool enough to handle, break each walnut into 2–3 pieces and set aside.

Melt the butter in the same pan over a medium heat, then add the cinnamon. When the butter starts to foam, add the pears and allow to sizzle for a minute. Add the honey and turn up the heat to high so the pears start to caramelize until they soften but still retain their shape – this should take no more than 4–5 minutes. Turn off the heat and leave the pears in the pan.

When ready to serve, reheat the pear caramel and spoon over the pancakes. Top with a scoop of vanilla ice cream and sprinkle over the toasted walnuts.

"The PBJ"

PBJ pops up in many of my recipes and dishes at the restaurant in different guises. It's such a great combination, endorsed, of course, by the one and only Mr Presley. The crumbled shortbread adds a crunchy texture.

Serves 2
Preparation time: 10 minutes
Cooking time: 10 minutes

50ml (2fl oz) double cream
10g (¼oz) caster sugar
½ vanilla pod, seeds only
2 tablespoons peanut butter
4 American-style Pancakes
  (see page 88)
1 tablespoon strawberry jam
5–6 strawberries
1 shortbread biscuit

In a mixing bowl, whisk the cream, sugar and vanilla seeds together until the mixture forms soft peaks.

When ready to serve, "butter" each of the pancakes with the peanut butter, then spread over the jam. Give each one a good spoon of whipped cream, scatter the strawberries around, and finish by crumbling the shortbread biscuit and scattering over the top.

Toffee apple, mascarpone, granola crumble (*pictured on page 102*)

If you're pushed for time, shop-bought granola is fine, but I have included a recipe here that makes about a kilo. It's great to have in the cupboard for breakfast treats – or you can halve or quarter the quantities to make less.

Serves 2
Preparation time: 10 minutes
Cooking time: 40 minutes if making granola; 10 minutes if not

20g (¾oz) demerara sugar
2 apples, peeled, cored and cut into 8 wedges
4 American-style Pancakes (see page 88)
2 tablespoons mascarpone cheese
70g (2½oz) Granola (see below)
20g (¾oz) butter

Granola (Makes about 1kg/2lb 4oz)
500g (1lb 2oz) oats
100g (3½oz) hazelnuts
100g (3½oz) almonds
50g (1¾oz) pistachios
50g (1¾oz) cashews
100g (3½oz) walnuts
25g (1oz) sesame seeds
25g (1oz) sunflower seeds
25g (1oz) pumpkin seeds
125g (4½oz) golden syrup
100g (3½oz) maple syrup
60g (2¼oz) cranberries
60g (2¼oz) raisins
60g (2¼oz) dried apricots
60g (2¼oz) prunes

To make the granola, preheat the oven to 160°C fan/350°F/gas mark 4.

Mix all the granola ingredients, except the dried fruit, and divide between 2 large baking tray lined with baking paper. Bake, giving a mix every 10 minutes so, for about 30 minutes or until everything becomes evenly coloured. Remove from the oven, mix in the dried fruit and set aside to cool.

Heat a frying pan over a medium heat and add the sugar. As the sugar starts to caramelize, throw in the apples and give them a stir. Allow the apples to cook in the caramel for 3–4 minutes, until they soften but still retain a slight bite. Add the butter and allow it to melt and bubble, making a sauce around the apples. Turn off the heat.

To serve, spoon the toffee apples over the pancakes, add a spoonful of mascarpone and sprinkle with the granola. The mascarpone will start to melt into the toffee apples and make a gorgeous cream.

Rhubarb & custard (*pictured overleaf*) Rather than traditional runny hot custard, here I use the French crème pâtissière, which you'll know from custard doughnuts and the like. It's firmer, and when spooned on to freshly cooked pancakes it takes the heat, but softens enough to make a cream around the rhubarb. This recipe makes four portions rather than two like other recipes in this chapter, as it is easier to make the rhubarb and custard in slightly larger quantities.

Serves 4
Preparation time: 10 minutes
Cooking time: 30 minutes

8 American-style Pancakes
  (see page 88)

Crème pâtissière
250ml (9fl oz) milk
400ml (14fl oz) double cream
1 vanilla pod, seeds only
1 egg
3 egg yolks
50g (1¾oz) cornflour
125g (4½oz) caster sugar

Poached rhubarb
1kg (2lb 4oz) rhubarb, peeled
  and sliced into 1cm (½ inch)
  thick pieces
75g (2¾oz) caster sugar
1 star anise

The crème pâtissière should be made in advance, as it needs time to cool. In a large pan, heat the milk, cream and vanilla seeds to just below boiling point. Meanwhile, mix the egg, egg yolks, cornflour and sugar in a large bowl.

When the milk mix is hot, pour slowly over the egg mix while whisking. Return the mixture to the pan and reduce the heat to low. Stir until it thickens to a mayonnaise-like consistency, taking care that it doesn't catch on the base of the pan or scramble. Pass the mixture through a sieve, using a dough scraper to push it through, which will result in a thick, silky custard. Put a layer of clingfilm directly on top so a skin doesn't form and set aside to cool.

Next, place the rhubarb in a pan with the sugar, star anise and enough water to just cover. Bring to the boil, then reduce the heat and simmer for 10 minutes. Strain and set aside to cool. Save the strained syrup, and reduce over a low heat until it reaches a honey-like consistency. Allow to cool, and we'll use this as a sauce.

To serve, spoon a good dollop of the crème pâtissière on each pancake, and top each one with a spoonful of the rhubarb. Finish by drizzling the syrup all over.

Coconut pancakes with rum-roasted pineapple The combination of rum, pineapple and coconut makes so much sense to me, even on a pancake. I add vanilla ice cream too because, well, why not...?

Serves 2
Preparation time: 10 minutes
Cooking time: 10 minutes

80g (2¾oz) desiccated coconut
4 American-style Pancakes
  (see page 88)
4–5 fresh mint leaves, finely sliced
2 scoops of Vanilla Ice Cream
  (see page 97)

Rum roasted pineapple
50g (1¾oz) dark, soft brown sugar
100g (3½oz) pineapple, peeled
  and cut into 2cm (¾ inch) dice
50ml (2fl oz) rum
20g (¾oz) butter

In a frying pan over a medium heat, gently toast the desiccated coconut until golden brown. Transfer to a bowl or plate and leave to cool. When completely cold, add three-quarters of it to the pancake mix and stir in.

Put the sugar into another frying pan over a medium heat and leave it to caramelize. When bubbling and brown, add the pineapple pieces and sauté in the caramel for 2–3 minutes, or until softened but not completely stewed. Add the rum and give the pan a little shake. It'll be bubbling away by this point. Add the butter and simmer until it gets to a toffee sauce like consistency. Turn off the heat and leave it on the stove.

Stir the mint into the rum roasted pineapple and spoon over the pancakes. Serve with the ice cream, and sprinkle over the remaining toasted coconut.

Strawberry, chocolate, almond & biscuit crumble pancake wraps

The crêpe has one great advantage over American-style pancakes; it's wrapable. Layer up homemade chocolate and almond spread with strawberries and a crunchy biscuit crumble on freshly cooked pancakes, then wrap them up and get messy.

Makes 4
Preparation time: 20 minutes
Cooking time: 10 minutes

4 tablespoons Homemade
   Chocolate & Almond Spread
   (see page 15)
10–12 strawberries, tops removed
   and sliced ½cm (¼ inch) thick
3 shortbread biscuits, smashed to
   a crumble

Pancake batter
20g (¾oz) butter
130g (4¾oz) plain flour
1 egg
300ml (½ pint) milk
sunflower oil, for cooking

To make the pancake batter, melt the butter, and allow to cool to around room temperature. Put the flour, egg and milk in a bowl, whisk together, then stir in the butter.

Heat a non-stick frying pan over a medium heat and add a teaspoon of oil. When the oil is hot, add a ladleful of the pancake batter and quickly tilt the pan to spread the batter to the edges of the pan, leaving no gaps. After 30 seconds on the heat the pancake should be set. Turn the pancake over, using a palette knife (or flip if you're confident) and cook for another 30 seconds on the other side. Remove to a plate and repeat the process with the remaining oil and batter.

To serve, spread a spoonful of chocolate and almond spread over each pancake, scatter the strawberries over and sprinkle on some of the biscuit crumble. Wrap, eat, repeat.

HANGOVER

5

Cooking with a hangover can be a terrifying thing. However, there is no denying it – if you manage to cook your cure of choice, you'll feel substantially better. Grilling bacon and frying an egg can feel like you're defusing a bomb, but I do think it's all worth it.

So how can we make our lives easier and our recovery quicker? We can be organized and plan for our hangover which sounds ridiculous but makes so much sense. Think of waking up with a splitting headache and reheating some smoky bacon sloppy Joes within 5 minutes? It's a game changer, but I'm not sure it's the solution. The problem with that method is twofold. First, when sitting in a beer garden, loving life, I never think I will actually get a hangover and I never learn. Second, most nights are spontaneous; I'm not going to pop home and cook for an hour when we decide to go out for a few beers.

The compromise I have found is leftovers. Taking something you've cooked with love, and turning it into a healing hangover dish is the way forward, believe me. The hard work has been done – you just need to put the pieces together and get eating.

The hashes in this chapter are great examples of how quickly you can turn some leftover roasties and a bit of meat into a tasty breakfast feast. You can use leftover pork in a rösti, reheat some stew and serve it with quick cheesy polenta or transform your leftover cheeseboard into rarebit. Not everyone's cures are the same, but if you use the ingredients you have available you'll be able to make and enjoy good food more quickly, so you can crack on with planning the next night out...

PS: This chapter is HANGOVER, so don't go judging me if ingredients are shop-bought – that's the point.

Blue cheese, English mustard & onion jam rarebit

Cheese on toast needs no introduction and nor does a good rarebit. I add onion jam to mine, which is fine to buy – you can find it in plenty of shops. Cheese and onion is a match made in heaven, so it made sense to get it in here somehow.

Makes 6 slices
Preparation time: 10 minutes
Cooking time: 20 minutes

150ml (¼ pint) brown ale
1 teaspoon English mustard
2 tablespoons Worcestershire sauce
25g (1oz) butter
25g (1oz) plain flour
150ml (¼ pint) milk
175g (6oz) Stilton cheese, cut into
   1cm (½ inch) cubes
sea salt flakes and freshly ground
   black pepper
2 egg yolks
2 tablespoons onion jam
6 slices of sourdough bread

Put the ale, mustard and Worcestershire sauce into a medium saucepan and bring to the boil. Simmer until reduced by half.

Meanwhile, in another medium saucepan, melt the butter on a medium heat. Stir in the flour – the mixture will resemble a wet sand consistency. Keep stirring on the heat for 2–3 minutes, then slowly add the milk while stirring. If the mixture gets a little lumpy you can use a whisk to smooth it out.

Add the Stilton and mix in, then add the reduced beer to the cheesy mix and take the pan off the heat. Season with salt and pepper, then stir in the egg yolks and the onion jam.

Turn on your grill to medium. Toast the bread on both sides and put the slices on a baking tray. Using a palette knife or the back of a spoon, spread the rarebit mix liberally over all the slices.

Grill for a minute or two, until it browns and bubbles.

Ultimate grilled cheese sandwich

Ultimate grilled cheese sandwich One of the greatest American exports, the grilled cheese sandwich, is naughty but it's a winner. Use any cheese you want. I recommend Swiss, American or Cheddar, but use whatever you have (nothing too strong or hard like Parmesan, though). The bacon is optional but, in my eyes, totally necessary and the bread you use shouldn't be anything fancy. Seedy wholemeal here is just wrong – white bloomer is the way forward.

Makes 2
Preparation time: 5 minutes
Cooking time: 15 minutes

40g (1½oz) butter
4 slices of white bread
4 slices of cheese
6 rashers of streaky bacon, grilled until crisp
2 tablespoons onion jam
2 eggs

Butter the bread on both sides (saving a knob of butter for cooking the eggs later on), and lay the cheese on 2 of the slices. Arrange the bacon on top of the cheese, then spread the onion jam on the remaining slices and sandwich them on top of the bacon to make 2 sandwiches.

Heat a frying pan over a low heat. The trick here is to cook the sandwiches slowly, so that by the time the bread is brown the cheese is already on its way to melting. Too quick, and the bread will burn before your cheese is ready.

Put the first sandwich into the pan (or both, if your pan is big enough) and cook for 2–3 minutes. Using a palette knife, lift up the sandwich and have a peek underneath – the base should be golden brown, and the cheese inside just beginning to melt. Turn over and repeat the process. Again, the base should be golden brown and now, inside, the cheese should have melted. Take the sandwich out of the pan, put it on a plate and allow it to cool for a few minutes. Cook the second sandwich the same way if you have not cooked both together.

While the sandwich is cooling, fry the eggs, using the remaining butter, then crown your grilled cheese sandwiches with a fried egg each, and get stuck in.

Potato waffle, bacon, egg & maple syrup throw-down

As a kid I was addicted to potato waffles. Breakfast, lunch or dinner with sausages and beans – I was a happy boy. Potato waffles lend themselves really well to sandwiches; the crisp potato is the perfect vehicle for all kinds of naughtiness.

Makes 2
Preparation time: 5 minutes
Cooking time: 10 minutes

6 potato waffles
4 streaky bacon rashers, grilled until crisp
4 slices of easy-melting cheese
4 eggs
25g (1oz) butter
1 small piece of red onion, finely sliced
50ml (2fl oz) maple syrup
tomato ketchup, or sauce of your choice

Preheat the oven to 160°C fan/350°F/gas mark 4.

Cook your waffles in a toaster or in the oven – they should take 4–5 minutes.

When they are cooked, place 4 waffles on an oven tray and top each with a layer of bacon, then cheese. Pop into the oven for 2 minutes, or until the cheese melts.

In the meantime, fry your eggs in the butter.

When the cheese has melted, take the waffles out of the oven, add some red onion slices and place an egg on each. Build 2 sandwiches by placing one loaded waffle on top of another, then top with a final waffle. Drizzle with maple syrup all over. Serve with the sauce of your choice on the side.

Cheesy polenta with leftover meat stew This isn't really a recipe per se, more a serving suggestion. I wouldn't ever imply that making a stew for a hangover breakfast is the way to go – it's too much work and you'll need a cure before the three hours it will take to make it. However, if you have a tub of stew in the fridge left over from a day or two earlier, this is great comfort food to blow out the sadness a hangover brings.

Serves 2
Preparation time: 5 minutes
Cooking time: 20 minutes

100g (3½oz) quick-cook polenta
milk, for cooking the polenta
   (check the packet instructions)
150g (5½oz) leftover meat stew
20g (¾oz) butter
40g (1½oz) Parmesan cheese,
   grated, plus extra grated cheese
   to serve

To cook the polenta, follow the packet instructions, using the milk as instructed.

While the polenta is cooking, reheat your leftover stew, with a splash of water or stock to loosen it.

When the polenta is ready, stir in the butter and cheese. The mixture should be nice and soft.

Serve the polenta in a bowl with a good ladleful of stew in the middle and more grated Parmesan on top.

The Scotch bhaji

My favourite hybrid, combining the worlds of Scotch eggs and onion bhajis. It has everything – subtle spice, crispiness, pork and a runny egg.

Makes 6
Preparation time: 10 minutes
Cooking time: 10 minutes

a pinch of salt
6 eggs
20g (¾oz) plain flour

Scotch egg mix
250g (9oz) sausage meat
1 garlic clove, finely chopped
1 small red chilli, finely chopped
10g (¼oz) onion powder
a pinch of finely chopped fresh
  coriander
10g (¼oz) finely grated ginger
1 egg yolk

Bhaji mix
60g (2¼oz) chickpea flour
60g (2¼oz) plain flour
1 teaspoon garam masala
1 teaspoon garlic powder
1 teaspoon onion powder
¼ teaspoon cayenne pepper
½ teaspoon ground turmeric
½ teaspoon ground cumin
½ teaspoon ground ginger
2 onions, finely sliced

Bring a pan of water to the boil and add a pinch of salt. Boil the eggs for 6 minutes. When cooked, remove and refresh in ice-cold water. When cool, shell the eggs and set them aside.

For the Scotch egg mix, combine all the ingredients in a bowl and keep in the fridge.

For the bhaji mix, put all the ingredients into a bowl and mix together, stir in just enough cold water to produce a thick, smooth batter.

Preheat a deep-fat fryer to 160°C (325°F).

To assemble the bhajis, take a ball of Scotch egg mix roughly the size of an egg. Flatten it out, then wrap it around one of the soft-boiled eggs. Put the coated egg on a plate and repeat with the remaining Scotch egg mix and eggs.

Roll each Scotch egg in flour and dust off the excess. Drop into the bhaji mix, then, using your hands, lift out and carefully lower into the fryer. The onions will spread out and look messy, but that's fine. Fry them 2 at a time for 8 minutes, then remove from the fryer and put on a plate lined with kitchen paper to drain the excess oil.

Baked Camembert, Marmite cheese straws

You can't beat a pot of runny cheese with some crisp pastry to dip in. As an ingredient, Marmite adds a lovely meaty undertone to things and has lots of umami going on too. If you don't like Marmite, simply leave it out.

Serves 2
Preparation time: 30 minutes
Cooking time: 10 minutes

100g (3½oz) puff pastry
2 tablespoons Marmite
1 teaspoon water
50g (1¾oz) Parmesan cheese, finely grated
1 small 250g (9oz) Camembert cheese

Preheat the oven to 180°C fan/400°F/gas mark 6.

On a floured work surface, roll out the puff pastry to a thickness of approximately 2mm (¹/₁₆ inch) – it should be the size of an A4 sheet of paper. Pop the rolled-out pastry into the freezer to firm up for 10 minutes.

Meanwhile, gently heat the Marmite in a small saucepan with a teaspoon of water. Take the pastry out of the freezer and, using a pastry brush, brush it with the warm Marmite. Cut strips from the pastry that are 1cm (½ inch) wide.

Line a baking tray with baking paper, and place the pastry strips on the tray, leaving 1cm (½ inch) gaps between them. Sprinkle Parmesan over each strip; it should stick to the Marmite. Now, twist each strip so it folds over itself into a spiral.

Remove any wrapping from the Camembert and place it on a baking tray. If it came in a little wooden box, put it back in the box, then put the box on the baking tray. Bake the cheese and the straws for 10 minutes, or until the pastry is crisp and golden brown, and the cheese is nicely melted.

Pulled pork rösti, eggs & chipotle (*pictured on page 126*) This recipe offers

a great way to use up leftover roast pork. If you want to make it from scratch, I have included a recipe for a roast pork belly below. If you do have a chunk left over, simply heat it in an oven at 160°C fan/350°F/gas mark 4 for about 20 minutes, then pull the meat apart using two forks moving in opposite directions. Serve any leftover crackling on the side.

Makes 2

Preparation time: 20 minutes, plus resting time if roasting the pork

Cooking time: 3½ hours if roasting the pork, 20 minutes if not

Rösti

2 potatoes, cooked halfway, then peeled

1 tablespoon chipotle paste

a handful of leftover pulled pork (or see below)

olive oil

1 onion, finely diced

a pinch of finely chopped fresh coriander

sea salt flakes and freshly ground black pepper

40g (1½oz) butter

2 eggs

a few stalks of fresh chives, finely chopped

Pork belly

1 onion, peeled and quartered

3 garlic cloves, crushed with skin on

1 carrot, peeled and halved lengthways

2 bay leaves

1 sprig of fresh thyme

2 sprigs of fresh sage

500g (1lb 2oz) pork belly, skin scored

olive oil

sea salt flakes and freshly ground black pepper

400ml (14fl oz) chicken stock

For the pork belly, if you are roasting it from scratch, preheat your oven to 200°C fan/425°F/gas mark 7.

Put the onion, garlic, carrot and herbs into a roasting tray and place the pork joint on top. Drizzle with olive oil and season well. Roast for about 30–45 minutes, or until a crackling begins to form, at which point then reduce the temperature to 160°C/140°C fan (325°F), gas mark 3.

Add the stock and continue roasting for another 2 hours or so, until the meat falls apart when pressed with a fork. If it dries out too much, top up with a little water.

Remove from the oven and leave to rest for 30 minutes. Then, using 2 forks move them in opposite directions and pull the meat apart – you need about a handful of pulled pork for this recipe.

To make the rösti, grate the potatoes and put into a mixing bowl. Add the chipotle paste and a handful of pulled pork and mix well.

Heat a frying pan and add a splash of olive oil. Add the onion and sauté over a medium heat for 3–4 minutes, taking care not to let it colour, then add it to the potatoes and pork. Add the coriander, season with salt and pepper and stir well.

Heat a small non-stick frying pan over a medium heat and melt half the butter. When it begins to foam, add half the rösti mix and spread it out evenly. Cook for 5–6 minutes, or until golden brown, then carefully turn it over and repeat the process. When cooked on both sides, slide the rösti out of the pan and on to a plate. Repeat with the remaining rösti mix and butter.

Heat another frying pan and fry the eggs. Serve each rösti with an egg seasoned with salt and pepper and a sprinkling of chopped chives.

Shakshouka with mint yoghurt & toasted buckwheat (*pictured overleaf*)

Of Tunisian origin, this is one of those one-pot wonders that I adore. Have all your ingredients prepared and you'll have a big pan of love ready to eat in less than half an hour.

Serves 4
Preparation time: 10 minutes
Cooking time: 25 minutes

50ml (2fl oz) yoghurt
a pinch of finely sliced fresh mint
olive oil, for cooking
½ onion, finely chopped
2 garlic cloves, finely chopped
1 bay leaf
1 red chilli, finely chopped
sea salt flakes and freshly ground
   black pepper
1 teaspoon cumin seeds, toasted
1 teaspoon smoked paprika
a pinch of cayenne pepper
1 red pepper, deseeded and sliced
   ½cm (¼ inch) thick
1 x 400g (14oz) can of chopped
   tomatoes
200ml (7fl oz) vegetable stock
a pinch of finely chopped
   fresh coriander
a pinch of finely chopped
   fresh parsley
4 eggs
30g (1oz) toasted buckwheat
mint leaves, to garnish

Mix the yoghurt and sliced mint together in a bowl and set aside.

Heat some olive oil in a large pan or casserole over a medium heat and sauté the onion, garlic, bay leaf and chilli for 3 minutes – if they become a little coloured, this is fine. Season with salt and pepper. Add the cumin, paprika and cayenne and cook for a further 3 minutes. Add the red pepper slices and cook for 5 minutes, or until they begin to soften.

Pour in the chopped tomatoes and stock, then lower the heat and simmer for 10 minutes. Stir in the coriander and parsley, then make 4 little wells in the surface of the sauce and crack one egg into each well. Simmer over a very low heat for 10 minutes, or until the eggs are set but still soft.

When ready, season the eggs with salt and pepper, sprinkle over the buckwheat and serve with dollops of the mint yoghurt and fresh mint leaves to garnish.

The patty melt A wonderful variation on a burger – this is the ultimate toastie. As is so common in my world an egg can easily make its way in too, along with some hot sauce.

Makes 2
Preparation time: 10 minutes
Cooking time: 40 minutes

4 slices of sourdough bread
250g (9oz) minced beef
sea salt flakes and freshly ground
　black pepper
olive oil
4 slices of Swiss cheese
1 tablespoon onion jam
2 large gherkins, sliced 2mm
　(1/16 inch) thick
25g (1oz) butter

Preheat your grill. Toast the bread on one side (this will be the inside of your sandwich).

Put the minced beef into a mixing bowl and season well with salt and pepper. Take half the mince and mould and press it into a burger shape with your hands. Repeat with the remaining mince.

Heat a frying pan over a high heat and add a splash of olive oil. When the oil is hot, add the burgers and cook until nicely seared – this should take 2 minutes on each side.

Remove the burgers from the pan and set aside.

To build your sandwiches, lay a slice of cheese on all 4 slices of bread (the toasted side). Put the 2 burgers on top of 2 of the cheese toasts. Add some onion jam and sliced gherkins on top of the burger, then top with the remaining slices of bread (cheese side down) and lightly press together.

Heat a frying pan over a medium heat. Add the butter and let it melt and foam, then add the sandwiches. Cook for 2–3 minutes on each side, or until nice and golden brown – the cheese should be melting inside, too.

Breakfast tacos Eating spicy food is my way to blow out a hangover. Putting breakfast stuff into a taco shell is an obvious thing to me; add the spice and that hangover will soon be gone.

Makes 4
Preparation time: 10 minutes
Cooking time: 10 minutes

1 teaspoon chipotle paste
1 tablespoon tomato ketchup
2 chorizo sausages, skin removed, cut into 1cm (½ inch) cubes
4 eggs
sea salt flakes and freshly ground black pepper
a pinch of finely chopped fresh coriander
4 ready-to-eat taco shells
30g (1oz) grated Cheddar cheese
2 spring onions, finely sliced on an angle

Mix the chipotle paste and ketchup together in a bowl and set aside.

Fry the chorizo over a medium heat and allow it to cook in its own oil for 3–4 minutes.

Meanwhile, crack your eggs into a bowl, add some salt and pepper and whisk together. Add to the pan of chorizo and scramble together – the eggs should be cooked within 3 minutes. Stir in the coriander.

Spoon the egg mix into the taco shells. Top each taco with some grated Cheddar and sliced spring onion.

Serve with ½ teaspoon of the chipotle sauce on each one and eat straight away.

Chicken & waffles This dish inspired the Duck & Waffle, and what a dish it is – humble, comforting and, most importantly, healing, I truly love cooking and eating this old classic – it makes the best brunch. Whenever I'm in the States I make a point of finding the local fried chicken spot.

Serves 4
Preparation time: 8 hours including marinating,
30 minutes without
Cooking time: 15 minutes

4 chicken legs, jointed (or 4 thighs and 4 drums)
salt
vegetable oil, for oiling
maple syrup, to serve

Marinade
100ml (3½fl oz) buttermilk
a pinch of sea salt flakes
a pinch of freshly ground black pepper
a pinch of chilli flakes

Crust
200g (7oz) plain flour
1 teaspoon paprika
a pinch of cayenne pepper
1 teaspoon onion powder
1 teaspoon mustard powder

Waffle batter
180g (6oz) plain flour
15g (½oz) caster sugar
1 teaspoon baking powder
½ teaspoon bicarbonate of soda
a pinch of salt
340ml (12fl oz) buttermilk
60g (2¼oz) butter, melted
1 egg

Mix all the marinade ingredients together in a bowl and massage the mix into the chicken. Leave in the fridge for at least 8 hours to marinate.

Mix together all the ingredients for the crust.

For the waffle batter, mix together the flour, sugar, baking powder, bicarbonate of soda and salt in a bowl. Whisk together the buttermilk, melted butter and egg in another bowl, then whisk this into the flour mixture until just combined. The batter will be quite thick, which is perfectly normal. Store in the fridge until needed.

Before cooking the chicken, take it out of the fridge for an hour to allow it to come back up to room temperature. Preheat a deep-fat fryer to 160°C (325°F). Take the chicken pieces out of the buttermilk, scraping off all the excess marinade. Roll the chicken in the crust mixture to coat all over, then carefully lower the chicken pieces into the oil and deep-fry for 12 minutes, or until golden brown.

When cooked and crispy, remove the chicken from the fryer and strain on a rack for 2 minutes, then transfer to a plate lined with kitchen paper. Season with salt.

To make your waffles, turn on your waffle iron. Brush the hot waffle iron with oil and pour a ladleful of batter into each waffle mould, spreading it all around, as the mix is quite thick and won't spread on its own. Cook until golden and cooked through, about 3 minutes.

Serve a leg and a drum per waffle, with a good splash of maple syrup.

Smoky bacon sloppy Joes

Smoky bacon sloppy Joes More American comfort food! Although included here in the hangover chapter, this dish is also well suited to a late-night feast before a hangover kicks in. Try crunching a bag of crisps over the top for a bit of texture.

Makes 4
Preparation time: 10 minutes
Cooking time: 20 minutes

8 rashers of smoked streaky bacon, cut into ½cm (¼ inch) strips
300g (10½oz) minced pork
2 onions, finely diced
2 garlic cloves, finely chopped
2 bay leaves
sea salt flakes and freshly ground black pepper
2 teaspoons Harissa (see page 171)
40g (1½oz) tomato purée
200ml (7fl oz) chicken stock
200g (7oz) tomato ketchup
a pinch of finely chopped fresh parsley
4 hot dog buns

To make the sloppy Joe mix, heat a pan over a medium heat and fry the bacon for about 5 minutes, or until the natural fat is released and the bacon becomes nice and brown.

Add the pork and let it brown in the bacon fat for 4–5 minutes. Add the onions, garlic and bay leaves and cook for a further 3 minutes, or until they are soft. Season with salt and pepper.

Stir the harissa and tomato purée into the sloppy Joe mixture, then stir in the chicken stock. Reduce the heat and simmer for 15 minutes, then stir in the ketchup and parsley.

To serve, slice each hot dog bun vertically and divide the sloppy Joe mix between them.

SAVOURY

6

I've always leaned more towards savoury food over sweet, especially when cooking. Whether it's comforting pork and prune meatballs or a big pot of feijoada, I love cooking this type of real food. The fun part for me is buying the ingredients the day before at a local market. I love seeing a table with the finished results to get stuck into – picture a lazy Sunday afternoon.

The recipes in this chapter are less dependent on your cooking skills and more about time. While the food is cooking and there isn't much left to do, your mates come over, the football is on, beers are opened and, as soon as you've watched your team lose (as is often the case in my life), the best part of the day has arrived. Sleeves are rolled up and all of a sudden the talking stops. The silence of a happy table is something so special.

This, to me, is what cooking is all about and, of course, it can be achieved with a good dessert too, but sweet things do always taste better after eating something savoury.

Sticky cornbread with grilled prawns & tomato salsa

This South American-inspired recipe is great for a garden party. If you have a barbecue on the go, cook the prawns and grill the cornbread on that, otherwise a griddle pan on the stove is fine. I prefer my prawns cooked in the shell; they taste better and the reward after I've peeled them is totally worth it. If you can't find them in the shell, peeled ones are OK, just cook them for a minute less. This is the kind of dish where you need to get messy, so have kitchen paper at the ready and get stuck in.

Serves 4
Preparation time: 1 hour
Cooking time: 45 minutes

8 tiger prawns (or the biggest
    prawns you can find), unpeeled
olive oil
20g (¾oz) butter
½ lemon
a pinch of salt

Cornbread
300g (10½oz) cornmeal, coarsely
    ground
2 tablespoons bacon fat
2 teaspoons bicarbonate of soda
1 teaspoon salt
1 tablespoon sugar
2 eggs, beaten
300ml (½ pint) buttermilk
4 tablespoons butter, melted
8 tablespoons maple syrup
½ teaspoon chilli flakes

Tomato salsa
2 plum tomatoes, quartered,
    deseeded and chopped into 1cm
    (½ inch) dice
½ a red onion, finely chopped
1 small green chilli, deseeded and
    finely chopped
1 lime, zest and juice
2 tablespoons olive oil
a pinch of chopped fresh coriander
a pinch of chopped fresh parsley
sea salt flakes and freshly ground
    black pepper

First, make the tomato salsa. Mix all the ingredients together and leave at room temperature for 1 hour for the flavours to develop.

To make the cornbread, gently toast the cornmeal in a frying pan over a low heat. Put into a bowl and leave to cool.

Preheat your oven to 200°C fan/425°F/gas mark 7. Put the bacon fat into a 23cm (9 inch) metal skillet and place in the oven to melt and heat for around 10 minutes.

Mix the cornmeal, bicarbonate of soda, salt, sugar, eggs and buttermilk in a mixing bowl. Stir in the melted butter.

Remove the skillet from the oven and place it on the stovetop. Pour in your cornbread batter (it should sizzle). Bake for approximately 20 minutes, or until golden brown and a skewer comes out clean when inserted in the middle. Take out of the oven and immediately drizzle over the maple syrup and sprinkle with the chilli flakes while it is still hot. Set aside in the skillet to rest.

Put the prawns in a bowl, drizzle over some olive oil and toss to coat them all with oil. If you are using tiger prawns, heat a griddle pan over a medium heat. When the pan is hot, add the prawns and grill for 2 minutes on each side. Don't worry if they burn a little, that's totally fine. When the second side is cooked, add the butter and allow it to foam around the prawns for 1 minute.

If you are using giant Madagascan prawns (as pictured), place them in a roasting pan and cook them under a hot grill for 7–8 minutes. Add the butter to the pan for the last minute.

When the prawns are ready, put them into bowl and pour over all the butter from the pan too. Add a squeeze of lemon juice and a pinch of salt and toss in the buttery juices.

Serve the cornbread with the bowl of prawns and the salsa on the side.

Leftover chicken congee, ginger, spring onion & runny eggs

Probably my preferred way of using up leftover chicken, congee is a wonderfully comforting dish. Found all over Asia, it's a staple in many cultures and you'll see why when you taste it. I cook my rice in chicken stock, made from a leftover roast chicken carcass, to intensify the flavour, but traditionally water is used.

Serves 2
Preparation time: 15 minutes
Cooking time: 30 minutes

2 eggs
100g (3½oz) sushi rice
500ml (18fl oz) chicken stock
sea salt flakes and freshly ground black pepper
a 2cm (¾ inch) piece of ginger, finely sliced
100g (3½oz) shredded cooked chicken
20g (¾oz) butter
2 sprigs of fresh coriander, chopped
1 spring onion, finely sliced
25g (1oz) roasted hazelnuts, crushed
2 tablespoons soy sauce
2 tablespoons Sriracha sauce

Boil the eggs for 5 minutes, then refresh them in cold water and remove the shells. Set aside.

Wash the rice under cold running water until the water turns clear and doesn't look milky. Put the washed rice into a pan with the chicken stock and simmer for 25 minutes, topping up the liquid as necessary. When the rice is cooked, season and stir in the ginger and the chicken. Leave to stand off the heat for 5 minutes. Add a drop of stock or water if it dries out.

When ready to serve, stir the butter into the rice until it's all melted and incorporated. Divide the rice between 2 bowls, and serve with a halved boiled egg on top, a good pinch of coriander, the spring onions and crushed hazelnuts. Drizzle over the soy and Sriracha sauces.

Grilled sea trout with potato, cucumber & grain mustard salad

It's best to cook the fish on a barbecue but if you don't have one a griddle pan is more than fine. I recommend making the salad a few hours in advance – the flavours will develop and only get better.

Serves 4
Preparation time: 10 minutes
Cooking time: 10 minutes

12–15 new potatoes
1 shallot, finely chopped
sea salt flakes and freshly ground
 black pepper
1 tablespoon wholegrain mustard
2 tablespoons white wine vinegar
olive oil, plus a splash
2 sprigs of fresh dill, finely
 chopped
1 cucumber
4 x 160g (5¾oz) fillets of sea trout
2 heads of baby gem lettuce, leaves
 separated and washed

Cook the potatoes in boiling salted water until tender, then let them cool a little and cut them into 5mm (¼ inch) thick slices. Set aside.

Heat a splash of olive oil in a frying pan, add the onions and cook gently for 3–4 minutes, or until soft. Season with salt and pepper.

Put the wholegrain mustard into a mixing bowl with the vinegar. Slowly whisk in 50ml (2fl oz) olive oil, so it emulsifies. Stir in the cooked onions and the dill.

Peel the cucumber, halve it lengthways, and scrape out and discard all the seeds, using a teaspoon. Slice it 2mm (¹/₁₆ inch) thick, then add it to the mustard dressing along with the potatoes and gently mix together. Put the salad into the fridge while you cook the trout.

To cook the fish, heat a griddle pan on a medium heat. Drizzle a little oil over the fish fillets and season with salt and pepper. Place on the grill and cook for about 4 minutes on each side. The cooking time will, of course, vary depending on the thickness of your fillets. When you press them with your finger, you should feel the flesh give a little.

When ready to serve, pop the fish on to plates, and make a nest with the gem leaves to the side. Spoon the potato and cucumber salad inside.

Honey-roast gammon, charred pineapple ketchup

I love gammon. Once you've cooked it, there are always at least two meals you'll get out of it. Be it a hash with the leftovers or a comforting pie the door is wide open to ideas. This way is great in a bread roll or try it in the Colcann-bac-on hash on page 76.

Serves 4
Preparation time: 20 minutes
Cooking time: 2½ hours

Gammon

1 carrot, peeled and sliced 2cm
 (¾ inch) thick
1 onion, peeled and sliced 1cm
 (½ inch) thick
2 garlic cloves, peeled and crushed
2 sprigs of fresh thyme
2 bay leaves
1 gammon joint, approx. 1kg
 (2lb 4oz), skin scored in a
 criss-cross pattern
olive oil
300ml (½ pint) chicken stock
10 cloves
100ml (3½fl oz) honey
Pineapple Ketchup, to serve
 (see below)

Pineapple ketchup

1 pineapple, peeled and cored,
 cut into 2cm (¾ inch) cubes
olive oil
1 onion, finely diced
2 garlic cloves, crushed
1 red chilli, halved, seeds left in
1 star anise
100g (3½oz) brown sugar
100ml (3½fl oz) white wine
 vinegar

Preheat your oven to 160°C fan/350°F/gas mark 4.

In a deep pot or roasting tray, arrange the carrot, onion, garlic, thyme and bay leaves and place the gammon on top, skin side up. As it has been cured, there is no need to season. Drizzle with olive oil, pour in the chicken stock and pop the joint into the oven to roast for 1 hour. Take the gammon out, baste with its juices, then roast for another hour, basting with its juices every 20 minutes.

Remove the meat from the oven and increase the oven temperature to 200°C fan/425°F/gas mark 7. Stick the cloves evenly all over the skin. Pour half the honey over the meat then return the joint to the oven. Keep an eye on it to avoid it burning, as the temperature is higher. After 5 minutes, take it out and pour over the remaining honey. After another 5 minutes, using a spoon, carefully spoon the honey and juices that have run off back over the meat. Repeat this process 2 or 3 more times until the gammon is nice and caramelized. Remove from the oven and put on a plate, then allow to rest for a good 30 minutes.

To make the ketchup, spread the pineapple out evenly on a roasting tray lined with baking paper, then roast in the oven at 200°C fan/425°F/gas mark 7 for about 30 minutes, or until the pineapple is almost burnt. (You can cook this at the same time as the gammon.)

While this is cooking, heat a pan over a medium heat, add a splash of oil and cook the onion, garlic, chilli and star anise for 5 minutes, taking care not to let them become coloured. When the pineapple is ready, add to the onion mix and stir it in. Add the sugar and vinegar, reduce the heat and simmer for 10–15 minutes, or until the mixture has reduced and thickened to a ketchup consistency. Leave to cool for 30 minutes, then discard the star anise and blitz the sauce in a blender until smooth.

To serve, slice the gammon and serve with a good splodge of Pineapple Ketchup and whatever sides take your fancy.

Pork & prune meatballs, mushroom gravy, Parmesan crumble

(*pictured on page 150*) Good meatballs are hard to beat – fact. They go with so many things too: bread, rice, mash, even the roasted squash on page 172. These balls can be made and rolled in advance, making this an easy winner for dinnertime.

Serves 4
Preparation time: 20 minutes
Cooking time: 20 minutes

Meatballs
olive oil
½ onion, finely chopped
2 garlic cloves, finely chopped
sea salt flakes and freshly ground
  black pepper
6 fresh sage leaves, finely chopped
300g (10½oz) minced pork
10 prunes, stoned and cut into
  ½cm (¼ inch) pieces
a pinch of finely chopped fresh
  parsley
50g (1¾oz) breadcrumbs

Mushroom gravy
olive oil
½ onion, finely chopped
1 garlic clove, finely chopped
1 bay leaf
1 sprig of fresh thyme
100g (3½oz) button mushrooms,
  finely sliced
sea salt flakes and freshly ground
  black pepper
50ml (2fl oz) white wine
200ml (7fl oz) chicken stock
200ml (7fl oz) double cream

To serve
10g (¼oz) butter
50g (1¾oz) breadcrumbs
50g (1¾oz) Parmesan cheese,
  grated

To make the meatballs, heat a medium pan on a medium heat and add a splash of olive oil. Add the onions and garlic and cook for 3–4 minutes, taking care not to let them colour. Season with salt and pepper and add the sage. Set aside to cool down.

Combine the minced pork, prunes, parsley, breadcrumbs and the cooled onion mix in a mixing bowl. Roll the mixture into balls approximately 2½cm (1 inch) in diameter, and set aside.

Now make the sauce. Heat a splash of olive oil in a medium pan on a medium heat and add the onion, garlic, bay leaf and thyme. Cook for 3–4 minutes, taking care not to let them colour. Add the mushrooms and cook for a further 5 minutes, or until all the juice has evaporated. Season with salt and pepper. Add the wine and reduce until almost dry, then add the stock and reduce by three-quarters. Add the cream and reduce by half.

Preheat your oven to 180°C fan/400°F/gas mark 6.

Heat some olive oil in a frying pan over a medium heat and sear the meatballs until golden brown. When nicely browned, put them into an ovenproof dish, pour over the mushroom gravy and bake for 10 minutes.

Meanwhile, melt the butter in a small saucepan. Add the breadcrumbs and cook on a low heat for 5–6 minutes, until golden. Add the Parmesan and cook for a further 2 minutes. When the meatballs are ready, scatter over the crumble and eat straight away.

Coronation haddock pie with carrot, fennel & raisin salad

(*pictured overleaf*) Pies are another British staple – one we should be very proud of. Here I have created a slight twist on a fish pie, using familiar Indian flavours to elevate the dish. Pies are known to be heavy so I've used pastry, rather than mashed potato, as a topping. I've served it with a light and vibrant salad.

Serves 4
Preparation time: 20 minutes
Cooking time: 30 minutes

1 egg, beaten
250g (9oz) ready-made puff pastry

Pie mix
olive oil
½ onion, finely diced
1 small carrot, finely diced
1 celery stick, finely diced
1 green chilli, deseeded and finely
  chopped
1 bay leaf
1 teaspoon curry powder
½ teaspoon cumin seeds
½ teaspoon coriander seeds
200ml (7fl oz) vegetable stock
200ml (7fl oz) double cream
400g (14oz) haddock, skinned and
  cut into 2cm (¾ inch) cubes
a few sprigs of fresh coriander,
  chopped
sea salt flakes and freshly ground
  black pepper

Salad
1 carrot, peeled
1 fennel bulb
1 apple, peeled, quartered and cored
50g (1¾oz) raisins
1 orange, peeled and cut into
  segments
40ml (1½fl oz) olive oil
20ml (¾fl oz) white wine vinegar
sea salt flakes and freshly ground
  black pepper
a few sprigs of fresh coriander,
  chopped

Preheat your oven to 180°C fan/400°F/gas mark 6. Have a pie dish ready, approximately 35 x 20cm (14 x 8in).

Heat a splash of olive oil in a medium pan on a medium heat. Add the onion, carrot, celery, chilli and bay leaf and cook for 6–7 minutes, taking care not to let them colour.

Put the curry powder, cumin seeds and coriander seeds in a dry frying pan over a medium heat and toast for a few minutes, shaking the pan, until you can smell the aromas and the spices look toasted.

When the vegetables are soft, stir in the toasted spices and season with salt and pepper. Add the vegetable stock and reduce by three-quarters, then add the cream and reduce by half. Turn off the heat, add the haddock and fresh coriander and gently stir in. Set aside for 5 minutes.

Pour the haddock mix into the pie dish and pop it into the fridge to cool down a little before putting the pastry on. There should be no steam coming off.

Using a pastry brush, brush the rim of the dish with the beaten egg. Roll out the pastry 3mm (⅛ inch) thick, about 25 x 20cm (10 x 8 inches or a little bigger than the dish you are using). Lay the sheet of pastry over the dish, then, using a fork, push down the edges to seal. Pop into the freezer for 10 minutes to allow the pastry to rest and firm up. Eggwash the pastry, then bake for 15 minutes, or until the pastry is golden brown.

In the meantime, make the salad. Grate the carrot, fennel and apple into a mixing bowl. Add the raisins, orange segments, olive oil, white wine vinegar and chopped coriander and season with salt and pepper. Give the salad a stir and set aside.

When the pie is ready, divide the pie between 4 plates and serve a good spoonful of salad on each.

Spicy sausage & lentil bake, kale & pickled walnuts

One-pot wonders are the way forward – less washing up and all that love kept in one place. Pickled walnuts are one of my go-to ingredients – they add a great tang to so many dishes and are readily available in most supermarkets.

Serves 2
Preparation time: 10 minutes
Cooking time: 15–20 minutes

olive oil
4 chorizo sausages
½ onion, finely sliced
1 garlic clove, finely sliced
1 small carrot, finely diced
2 bay leaves
sea salt flakes and freshly ground
    black pepper
100g (3½oz) Puy lentils, soaked
    overnight in cold water
300ml (½ pint) chicken stock
100g (3½oz) kale
4 pickled walnuts

Heat a splash of olive oil in a casserole over a medium heat, add the chorizo and sear on all sides. Set aside on a plate for later.

Add the onion, garlic, carrots and bay leaves to the casserole and cook for 5–6 minutes, taking care not to let them colour. Season with salt and pepper. Add the lentils, give them a stir, then add the stock and bring to the boil. Add the chorizo sausage, then reduce the heat and simmer for 10–15 minutes, or until the lentils are cooked and stew-like.

While the lentils are cooking, roughly chop the kale to cut it into smaller pieces. Slice the pickled walnuts 5mm (¼ inch) thick. When the lentils are cooked, add the kale to the casserole and stir over a low heat for 2–3 minutes until the kale is cooked.

Scatter over the pickled walnuts, then put the casserole in the middle of the table and dive in.

Feijoada, slow-cooked black beans with all the pork

This Portuguese/Brazilian classic – basically their answer to a cassoulet – is a great one-pot wonder with a load of pork involved. I've switched some of the traditional cuts, like pig's ears and trotters, for things that are more readily available. Some people add beef too; go ahead and use whatever you can get your hands on.

Serves 4-6
Preparation time: 20 minutes
Cooking time: 4 hours

1 smoked ham hock
2 litres (3½ pints) chicken stock, or enough to cover, depending on the size of your pan
300g (10½oz) pork belly, cut into 2cm (¾ inch) thick slices
500g (1lb 2oz) black beans, soaked overnight
olive oil
1 onion, finely chopped
2 carrots, finely chopped
1 celery stick, finely chopped
4 garlic cloves, crushed
2 bay leaves
1 sprig of fresh thyme
2 x 400g (14oz) cans chopped tomatoes
sea salt flakes and freshly ground black pepper
4 chorizo sausages
20g (¾oz) butter
100g (3½oz) breadcrumbs

Put the ham hock and chicken stock into a large pot on a medium heat, bring to the boil, then simmer for 2 hours. Skim off any foam or fat that rises to the surface. Top up with water or stock if needed. After the 2 hours are up, add the pork belly and the soaked beans.

Heat a splash of olive oil in a separate pan over a medium heat. Add the onion, carrots, celery, garlic and herbs and cook for 6–7 minutes, taking care not to let them become coloured. Add the canned tomatoes and bring to the boil. Season with salt and pepper. Add the contents of this pan to the pot of meat and beans and simmer for another hour, continuing to skim off any foam.

Add the sausages, and cook for another hour. By now the beans should be cooked. Turn off the heat, then carefully pick out and discard the herbs.

(You can slice the sausage and flake the ham hock at this stage and fold them back into the beans, or serve family style and all get stuck in.)

Heat the butter in a small pan on a medium heat and allow to foam. Add the breadcrumbs and toast until golden brown, stirring frequently.

Dish up the feijoada, and garnish with a sprinkling of the crumbs.

Whole roast chicken on potatoes, bacon & mushroom ragoût

More one-pot goodness; this is another Sunday favourite in my house. As the chicken roasts, the juices fall into the ragoût and make it even more flavoursome.

Serves 2–3
Preparation time: 20 minutes
Cooking time: 1 hour 20 minutes

1 large whole chicken, organic
    or free-range
olive oil
sea salt flakes and freshly ground
    black pepper
6 rashers streaky bacon, cut into
    1cm (½ inch) pieces
100g (3½oz) mixed mushrooms,
    cut into roughly 2cm (¾ inch)
    size pieces
10 new potatoes, cooked and halved
2 tablespoons onion jam
300ml (10fl oz) chicken stock
2 sprigs of fresh thyme
1 sprig of fresh rosemary
a few fresh parsley leaves
50g (1¾oz) butter

Preheat the oven to 160°C fan/350°F/gas mark 4.

Put the chicken into a roasting dish (breast side up). Drizzle a little olive oil over and season with salt and pepper. Roast for 30 minutes, or until it starts to colour.

Meanwhile, heat a pan over a medium heat and add a splash of olive oil. Add the bacon and cook for 5–6 minutes, or until it starts to colour and the fat is released. Add the mushrooms and cook for a further 5 minutes, until they soften. Add the potatoes, onion jam, chicken stock, thyme and rosemary and stir together. Bring to the boil, then pour into a large casserole.

Take the chicken out of the oven and carefully lift it out of the tray and on to the potato mix in the casserole – pour over all the juices too. Pop back into the oven for a further 30 minutes. When the cooking time is up, lift the chicken on to a plate to rest.

Put the casserole dish on the hob (or decant into a saucepan) and turn the heat to medium. When the juices come to the boil, allow to reduce by half, then add the parsley and the butter. Stir in so the butter melts and enriches the sauce. Turn off the heat and allow it to sit while you carve the chicken.

Cut the legs and the breast off the chicken, and cut each one in half. Place the chicken back on the potato ragoût and serve the casserole in the middle of the table.

SIDES
& SALADS

7

Vegetables are amazing. Truly. I'd have no issue whatsoever with being vegetarian. I think in the UK we have been slow to appreciate vegetables, aside from creating dishes solely aimed at vegetarians. What I mean by this is that in the past chefs have had to create dishes for people who don't eat meat or fish, but are now starting to realize that vegetables don't actually need meat or fish. They can certainly be enhanced by them, but it's not a necessity. Why can't carrots be the main focus of a dish, using lamb as a component? Well, we can cook like that, and we do.

I also feel that sides are often overlooked in menus. The classics are great – mash, chips, spinach and green beans – but you can be a little more creative too. Why not? To some, vegetables are an annoyance, something they feel they need to serve without thinking about them. This can stifle a home cook's imagination, as they only tend to cook the standard side dishes – there is little to be inspired by.

Go to your local farmers' market or greengrocer, and if you don't have access to either of those, go to a supermarket as their vegetable ranges are improving. Buy something you've never heard of or seen before and give it go. What's the worst that can happen?

If you've got a garden, you can even try growing them. They take a little work but the experience of eating something you've grown is unreal. It's what cooking is all about.

I hope this section of the book inspires you to get creative and show vegetables some love!

Sticky red onions, thyme, balsamic & mint

Goes great with roast leg of lamb or slow-braised beef (drop them in a sauce at the end for a lift).

Serves 2
Preparation time: 10 minutes
Cooking time: 45 minutes

2 red onions
50ml (2fl oz) olive oil
sea salt flakes and freshly ground
   black pepper
2 garlic cloves, crushed
2–3 sprigs of fresh thyme
1 tablespoon honey
50ml (2fl oz) balsamic vinegar
5–6 fresh mint leaves

Preheat the oven to 160°C fan/350°F/gas mark 4.

Trim the top and root off the onions and slice into 2cm (¾in) thick rounds. In a roasting tray, lay out the onion slices in one even layer. Drizzle over the olive oil, and season with salt and pepper. Scatter the garlic and thyme sprigs around, and put into the oven for 25 minutes. The onions should be starting to soften and colour by then. Take out, drizzle over the honey and balsamic, and put back into the oven for a further 20 minutes.

Meanwhile, finely slice the mint leaves. When the onions are ready, take them out and remove the thyme sprigs and scatter over the mint leaves. Give everything a stir to coat in the honey and balsamic glaze, then serve in a bowl.

Buttery mash

Mash is one of the greatest comfort foods around. It's integral to so many dishes – whether as a topping for pies or being served alongside them, as a base for other wonderful dishes such as colcannon or in a croquette. Mash is one of those foods that just makes you feel good when you eat it. This recipe is quite buttery and has thyme and nutmeg for subtle flavouring – you can, of course, add and take away as you please.

Serves 2
Preparation time: 10 minutes
Cooking time: 20 minutes

2 large potatoes, peeled and cut
   into 3cm cubes
sea salt flakes
50ml milk
20g butter
1 small sprig of fresh thyme
a grating of nutmeg
freshly ground black pepper

In a saucepan, add the potatoes and cover with cold water. Add a good pinch of salt and bring to a simmer.

In another pan, add the milk, butter and thyme. Grate in some nutmeg and add a few twists of black pepper. Heat gently, stirring, until the butter melts.

When the potatoes are cooked, drain well, then mash to a purée using a potato masher.

Remove the thyme sprig, then slowly stir the butter mix into the potato. Taste and adjust the seasoning if necessary.

Roasted root vegetables, creamed onions, garlic & crispy parsnips

(*pictured on page 167*) Goes great with roast leg of lamb, roast potatoes and buttered spring greens.

Serves 4–6
Preparation time: 15 minutes
Cooking time: 50 minutes

Roasted root vegetables
1 parsnip
1 swede
2 turnips
2 carrots
2 red onions
a sprig of fresh thyme
a sprig of fresh rosemary
3 garlic cloves, crushed
100ml (3½fl oz) olive oil
sea salt flakes and freshly ground
    black pepper

Creamed onions
olive oil
2 onions, finely sliced
sea salt flakes and freshly ground
    black pepper
300ml (10fl oz) double cream

Crispy parsnips
500ml (18fl oz) vegetable oil
1 parsnip
salt

Preheat the oven to 160°C fan/350°F/gas mark 4.

Peel all the root vegetables and cut them into roughly 3cm (1¼ inch) chunks. Cut the red onion into 2cm (¾ inch) thick wedges. Scatter the vegetables on a roasting tray, add the thyme, rosemary and garlic and drizzle the oil over. Give them a good mix with your hands and season with salt and pepper. Roast for approximately 45 minutes, until the vegetables are soft and nicely coloured.

While the vegetables are roasting, make the creamed onions. Put a small pan over a medium heat and add a splash of olive oil. Add the onions and cook for 8–10 minutes, until softened but not coloured. Season with salt and pepper, then add the cream and reduce by half. Transfer the mixture to a blender and blend until smooth, then set aside until you're ready to serve.

To make the crispy parsnips, put the vegetable oil into a pan over a medium heat. Peel the parsnip, then continue to peel it so you have long, thin slices of parsnip. Drop a piece of the parsnip into the oil; within 30 seconds it should be golden brown. If you have a thermometer, 180°C (356°F) is the temperature you're after. Carefully cook the parsnips in 2 or 3 batches, until golden brown, then lift out and drain on kitchen paper. Season with salt.

When ready to serve, reheat the onion purée and pour it into a large bowl. Pile the veggies on top, and finish with the crispy parsnips.

Wedge salad, bacon crumbs, blue cheese & buttermilk

(*pictured overleaf*) Goes great with traditional fried chicken and buttered grilled corn.

Serves 4
Preparation time: 10 minutes
Cooking time: 5 minutes

6 rashers of streaky bacon
1 iceberg lettuce, quartered,
  centre removed

Dressing
50g (1¾oz) blue cheese, crumbled
  into small pieces, plus extra for
  sprinkling
100ml (3½fl oz) buttermilk
2 tablespoons mayonnaise (to
  make your own, see page 171)
a pinch of finely chopped fresh
  chives
1 garlic clove, finely chopped
1 shallot, finely chopped
1 teaspoon French mustard
a few drops of Tabasco
sea salt flakes and freshly ground
  black pepper

Preheat a grill to medium, and grill the bacon on both sides until crisp. Allow to cool, then finely chop to a crumb consistency.

To make the dressing, whisk all the ingredients together and season with salt and pepper.

To serve, put a big spoon of dressing on each quarter of lettuce, cut side up, then sprinkle over some extra cheese and, finally, the bacon crumbs.

Curly kale, roasted garlic, chilli & hazelnuts Goes great with baked sea bass with roasted fennel and lemon.

Serves 2
Preparation time: 5 minutes
Cooking time: 35 minutes

3 garlic cloves, unpeeled
sea salt flakes and freshly ground
   black pepper
100g (3½oz) curly kale
2 tablespoons olive oil
1 red chilli, deseeded and finely
   sliced
½ lemon
large handful of hazelnuts, roasted
   and crushed

Preheat the oven to 180°C fan/400°F/gas mark 6.

Wrap the garlic cloves in foil, then put them on a small roasting tray. Roast for 25 minutes. Allow to cool, then unwrap and squeeze out the flesh from the skin. It will naturally have formed a purée. Set aside.

Bring a medium pan of water to the boil. Add a pinch of salt, then blanch the kale for 30 seconds, taking it out and refreshing in iced water. Drain well, then dry on a tea towel.

Heat a large frying pan, or a wok if you have one, over a medium heat. Add the olive oil and when hot add the blanched kale. Sauté for 2–3 minutes, then add the garlic and chilli and sauté together for 2 minutes. Season with salt and pepper, then place in a serving bowl.

Finely grate the zest of the lemon directly over and sprinkle the hazelnuts on top before serving.

Swiss chard, walnuts, golden raisins & anchovies

Goes great with grilled chicken marinated in garlic, thyme and chilli.

Serves 2
Preparation time: 10 minutes
Cooking time: 10 minutes

100g (3½oz) Swiss chard
2 tablespoons olive oil
½ onion, finely chopped
1 garlic clove, finely chopped
4 brown anchovy fillets
a sprig of fresh thyme
sea salt flakes and freshly ground
    black pepper
200ml (7fl oz) chicken stock
20g (¾oz) golden raisins
50g (1¾oz) walnuts, toasted and
    crushed, to garnish

Remove the leaves from the stems of the chard and set aside for later. Slice the stems 1cm (½ inch) thick.

Heat the olive oil in a large pan on a medium heat. Add the onion, garlic, anchovies and thyme and cook for 4–5 minutes, or until soft but without letting the onion colour. Season with salt and pepper. Take out the thyme, then add the chicken stock and reduce by half.

Add the raisins and the chard stems and cook for 3 minutes. Add the chard leaves and increase the heat to wilt the leaves quickly. Give everything a good stir. The stock should be nicely reduced and thickened to make a kind of sauce.

Serve in a bowl, finishing off with the walnuts on top, crushed slightly.

Fried artichokes with harissa mayo

This is food designed to go with a cold beer on a summer's day. Salty snacks with spicy mayo are just what I crave at times like this. You can make the whole thing much more quickly if you want to skip making the harissa and mayo, but I've included the recipes here if you want to make them yourself.

Serves 4

Preparation time: 20 minutes if making the mayo and harissa, 15 minutes if not

Cooking time: 30 minutes if making the mayo and harissa, 10 minutes if not

8 baby artichokes
500ml (18fl oz) corn oil
½ lemon, cut into wedges to garnish
sea salt flakes

Harissa

3 large red chillies
1 tablespoon coriander seeds
1 tablespoon cumin seeds
3 garlic cloves
1 tablespoon smoked paprika
50ml (2fl oz) olive oil
20ml (2fl oz) sherry vinegar
a pinch of salt
few sprigs of fresh coriander, chopped

Mayonnaise

2 egg yolks
1 tablespoon Dijon mustard
50ml (2fl oz) white wine vinegar
400ml (14fl oz) groundnut oil
sea salt flakes and freshly ground black pepper

First prepare the artichokes. Discard the outer leaves, cut the artichokes in half and remove the choke. Boil until tender, then drain well and leave to cool on kitchen paper.

To make the mayonnaise, whisk the egg yolks, mustard and vinegar together, either in a food processor or by hand. Now slowly start adding the oil. If the mix doesn't blend easily, slow down the speed a little. If the mix becomes too thick and excessively greasy, add warm water, a teaspoonful at a time until it loosens up a bit. Season with salt and pepper.

To make the harissa, preheat your oven to 180°C fan/400°F/gas mark 6. Put the chillies on a small baking tray and roast until blackened – this should take about 15 minutes. When they are cooked, put them into a mixing bowl and cover with clingfilm so the steam doesn't escape.

Meanwhile, put the coriander seeds and cumin seeds in a dry frying pan over a medium heat and toast for a few minutes, shaking the pan, until you can smell their aroma and they look toasted. Remove the seeds from the heat and grind or blend to a powder. Crush the garlic to a paste and put into a mixing bowl with the ground spices, then add the paprika.

When cool enough to handle, peel the skin off the chillies – it will come away easily. Cut the chillies in half lengthways and remove the seeds. Finely chop the chillies to a paste and add to the garlic. Add the olive oil, sherry vinegar, a pinch of salt and the chopped coriander and mix together well.

To make harissa mayo, take 3 tablespoons of mayo and 1 tablespoon of harissa and mix together. Set aside while you deep-fry the artichokes.

Heat the oil to 170°C (338°F) in a large saucepan. Carefully lower the artichokes into the oil and fry until golden brown, about 4 minutes, then take out and drain on kitchen paper. Season with salt.

Serve the fried artichokes with a wedge of lemon and a good spoon of harissa mayo on the side.

Roasted squash, spicy salami, feta & rocket

I love how the flavours of the salami melt into the squash as it roasts. The spiciness perfectly offsets the sweetness of the vegetable and the rocket and feta round it all off rather nicely. I think this is a dish in itself, but it would go really well with a roast chicken too.

Serves 4
Preparation time: 10 minutes
Cooking time: 55 minutes

50g (1¾oz) spicy salami,
   thinly sliced
100g (3½oz) feta cheese
1 handful of rocket

Squash
1 butternut squash
50ml (2fl oz) olive oil
sea salt flakes and freshly ground
   black pepper
1 sprig of fresh thyme
2 garlic cloves, crushed

Dressing
50ml (2fl oz) olive oil
20ml (¾fl oz) balsamic vinegar

Preheat the oven to 160°C fan/350°F/gas mark 4.

Halve and deseed the squash, then halve it lengthways again. Lay it cut side up on a roasting tray and drizzle over the olive oil. Season with salt and pepper and scatter over the thyme and garlic. Roast for about 45 minutes, or until the squash is cooked and nicely coloured.

When the squash is ready, remove and discard the thyme and garlic, and scatter over the salami. Roast for another 10 minutes, so the salami crisps up and the natural fats melt out on to the squash.

Remove from the oven and lift the squash slices on to a large sharing plate. Using your fingers, crumble over the cheese.

In a mixing bowl, mix together the oil and balsamic, then add the rocket and toss through. Serve the rocket on top of the squash.

Braised baby gem, pearl onions, peas & mint This is an old-school dish that isn't seen around much these days. "À la française" was a way of cooking peas at the end of the season, when they can be a bit tough. The peas are braised with baby onions in chicken stock, then finished with butter and flour to thicken, with a handful of shredded iceberg lettuce added at the end. I've always loved this dish, and I think it needs a revival. This is a slightly different version to the classic as I use baby gems and leave them in larger chunks for a bit of bite. Goes great with roast chicken.

Serves 2–4
Preparation time: 10 minutes
Cooking time: 20 minutes

10–12 pearl onions, peeled
1 bay leaf
1 sprig of fresh thyme
50g (1¾oz) butter
200ml (7fl oz) chicken stock
sea salt flakes and freshly ground
   black pepper
2 heads of baby gem lettuce, halved
2 handfuls of fresh peas
5–6 fresh mint leaves, finely sliced

Put the pearl onions, bay leaf, thyme, half the butter and the chicken stock into a medium pan. Season with salt and pepper and bring to the boil. Turn down the heat and simmer until the onions are tender – about 12 minutes.

Meanwhile, melt the remaining butter in a frying pan. When it is foaming, add the gem halves, cut side down and cook over a medium heat for about 3 minutes, or until golden brown. Turn over and colour the other side too. When browned, add the onions, pouring all the stock in too, and add the raw peas. Bring back to a simmer and cook for 8–10 minutes. The stock should be reduced almost to a sauce-like consistency.

When cooked, pick out the bay leaf, add the mint, stir through and serve right away.

Butterhead lettuce, broad beans, ricotta, pancetta croutons & mint

This is the kind of salad I like to make for a barbecue, where you have five or six dishes on the table for your friends and family to get stuck into. The ingredients are a classic combination found in Italian pasta and rice dishes, and they work great together as a salad too. Baby gem works well as a substitute here if you can't get hold of butterhead lettuce.

Serves 2–4
Preparation time: 10 minutes
Cooking time: 10 minutes

50g (1¾oz) pancetta, cut into
   1cm (½ inch) pieces
3 slices of white bread, cut into
   1cm (½ inch) cubes
50ml (2fl oz) olive oil
20ml (¾fl oz) white wine vinegar
100g (3½oz) fresh broad beans,
   cooked and peeled
5–6 fresh mint leaves, finely sliced
2 heads of butterhead lettuce,
   leaves separated and washed
sea salt flakes and freshly ground
   black pepper
2 tablespoons ricotta cheese

Preheat your oven to 160°C fan/350°F/gas mark 4.

Put the pancetta in an ovenproof frying pan or skillet over a medium heat and sauté for 4–5 minutes, or until the fat is released and the pancetta is golden brown. Add the diced bread and cook for another 3–4 minutes, so the bread absorbs the bacon fat and starts to get crunchy and golden too. Pop the pan into the oven for 5 minutes to finish off. When ready, set aside while you make the rest of the salad.

Mix the oil and vinegar together in a bowl and add the broad beans and the mint.

In a large salad bowl, toss together the lettuce leaves with the bacon and bread, and the broad bean mix. Season with salt and pepper and, using a teaspoon, spoon the ricotta around in 10–12 little dollops.

Middle Eastern-spiced roast vegetables, lentils, feta & mint salad

As well as being a great side, this works well as in a lunchbox too. Goes great with grilled lamb chops marinated in harissa.

Serves 2
Preparation time: 20 minutes
Cooking time: 45 minutes

1 parsnip
2 carrots
1 red onion
a sprig of fresh thyme
a sprig of fresh rosemary
a pinch of ground cinnamon
a pinch of cayenne pepper
a pinch of za'atar
3 garlic cloves, crushed
100ml (3½fl oz) olive oil
sea salt flakes and freshly ground
   black pepper
50g (1¾oz) green lentils, cooked as
   per packet instructions
50g (1¾oz) feta cheese
50ml (2fl oz) pomegranate
   molasses
a sprig of fresh coriander, roughly
   chopped, stalks included
5–6 fresh mint leaves, roughly
   chopped
olive oil, for drizzling

Preheat the oven to 160°C fan/350°F/gas mark 4.

Peel all the root vegetables and cut into roughly 3cm (1¼ inch) chunks. Cut the red onion into 2cm (¾ inch) thick wedges. Scatter on a roasting tray, then add the thyme, rosemary, spices and garlic and drizzle the oil over. Give them a good mix with your hands and season with salt and pepper. Roast for approximately 45 minutes, or until the vegetables are soft and nicely coloured.

When cooked, take them out of the oven and pick out the thyme and rosemary. Add the lentils, cheese, pomegranate molasses and herbs while still hot. Toss together and tip into a large salad bowl.
Finish with olive oil drizzled on top.

SWEETS

Queen of Puddings m
to me and I can't believe it
try it. I love the idea of br
custard – no doubt in the
to use up stale bread and s
base – then it is topped wi
classic French meringue.

In this chapter I think
of light desserts and comf
which I have enjoyed mak
past year or so. My waistli
they have all been tested –

A lot of the pudding
to make are either b
I remember eating w
or classics I've read
wanted to learn how
nostalgia that a jam
evoke is almost inde
making a Queen of
first time made me
don't see it on more

Rhubarb & ricotta tart Rhubarb is such a wonderful vegetable – its acidity lends itself to so many dishes, both sweet and savoury. This is a sweet tart, but using ricotta and shortcrust pastry does help give a lower overall sweetness, which I love.

Serves 8
Preparation time: 20 minutes
Cooking time: 25 minutes

butter, for greasing
1 sheet of ready-rolled shortcrust
    pastry, big enough for your
    tart case
500g (1lb 2oz) rhubarb, peeled
    and cut into 2cm (¾ inch) dice
200g (7oz) caster sugar
2 eggs
1 vanilla pod, seeds only
100ml (3½fl oz) double cream
200g (7oz) ricotta cheese
5–6 fresh basil leaves, to decorate

Preheat your oven to 160°C fan/350°F/gas mark 4. Grease a 25cm (10 inch) tart tin with butter.

Line the tart tin with the pastry. Lay a sheet of baking paper on top and fill with baking beans or rice. Bake until the exposed edges start to turn golden – this should take about 10 minutes. Remove the paper and beans, then bake for a further 6 minutes, until the base is golden brown too.

When ready, take out of the oven and reduce the temperature to 150°C fan/340°F/gas mark 3½.

Put the rhubarb into a medium pan with half the sugar and enough water to cover. Bring to the boil, then simmer until tender – about 6 minutes. Strain and set aside, discarding any juice.

Whisk the eggs with the remaining sugar and the vanilla seeds until well combined but not aerated. Add the cream and ricotta and stir in, mixing well. Pour the mix into the baked tart case and bake for about 25–30 minutes, or until just set but with a wobble. The mix should be set but still have a wobble. Leave to cool on a wire rack.

When the tart has cooled to room temperature, scatter over the poached rhubarb evenly, then scatter the basil over the top.

Banana bread French toast, maple-roasted apples & crème fraîche

I've never met anyone who doesn't like French toast which really says something. If you get the exterior nice and crunchy and the middle fluffy, you're on to a winner. I like to serve it with either fresh berries and cream, or more wintery apples in caramel, with the crème fraîche cutting through the richness nicely.

Makes a 1kg (2lb 4oz) loaf
Preparation time: 20 minutes
Cooking time: 45 minutes

50g (1¾oz) butter
2 apples, peeled, cored and cut
    into 2cm (¾ inch) wedges
100ml (3½fl oz) maple syrup
2 eggs, beaten
sunflower oil
50g (1¾oz) caster sugar
50g (1¾oz) crème fraîche

Banana bread
120g (4¼oz) butter, plus extra
    for greasing
140g (5oz) caster sugar
1 vanilla pod, seeds only
2 eggs, beaten
140g (5oz) self-raising flour
75ml (2½fl oz) buttermilk
2 ripe bananas, mashed

Preheat an oven to 180°C fan/400°F/gas mark 6. Grease a 1kg (1lb 2oz) loaf tin and line with baking paper.

First, make the banana bread. In a mixer, or using a mixing bowl and a wooden spoon, cream the butter and sugar with the vanilla seeds until light and fluffy. Slowly add the eggs and then fold in the flour. Fold in the buttermilk, then the bananas.

Pour in the cake mix and put it into the oven for approximately 30 minutes, or until a skewer inserted in the centre comes out clean. Cool in the tin on a wire rack, then turn out.

Heat a frying pan on a medium heat and add half the butter. When foaming, add the apples and sauté for 5–6 minutes, or until they take on a little colour. Add the maple syrup and reduce by half. Stir in the remaining butter to create a toffee-like sauce, then turn off the heat and set aside.

When the loaf is cool, slice off 4 slices, each about 2cm (¾ inch) thick. Put the beaten egg in a shallow bowl and soak the bread in the egg, pressing so the bread soaks up all the egg. Heat another frying pan on a medium heat, and add a splash of sunflower oil. When hot, fry the soaked banana bread on both sides until golden brown. Take out, and sprinkle each one with a pinch of caster sugar.

Using a blowtorch (or under a hot grill if you don't have one), caramelize the sugar on the outside of the toasts until golden brown, then pop them on to a plate for serving.

Spoon over the apples and finish with a good dollop of crème fraîche on each toast.

Lemon curd pavlovas Based on the classic with berries and cream, I use lemon curd instead for a refreshing tang. You can make your own meringue nests, if you like – follow the recipe on page 193 and pipe little mounds of meringue mixture on to a baking sheet lined with baking parchment, then bake in a preheated oven at 110°C/225°F/ gas mark ¼ for 2 hours, or until crisp. Turn off the oven and leave the oven door open to allow them to dry out until completely cold.

Serves 4–6
Preparation time: 10 minutes
Cooking time: 15 minutes

25g (1oz) caster sugar
1 vanilla pod, seeds only
100ml (3½fl oz) double cream
4–6 meringue nests
grated zest of 1 lemon

Lemon curd
4 eggs
350g (12oz) caster sugar
4 lemons, zest and juice
225g (8oz) butter, cut into 2cm
   (¾oz) cubes

To make the lemon curd, put the eggs, sugar, zest and juice into a mixing bowl set over a pan of simmering water. Whisk everything together continuously until the mixture thickens and becomes aerated. Beat in the butter, then transfer to a clean bowl. Cover the surface with a sheet of clingfilm to prevent a skin forming and set aside for later.

Whisk the sugar, vanilla and cream together until they form soft peaks.

Put a tablespoon of lemon curd in the centre of each meringue nest, cover with a spoonful of whipped cream and grate a little lemon zest over to finish.

Pear & almond frangipane tart (*pictured on page 190*) A simple, tasty dessert, with leftovers that make ideal elevenses the next day. Serve with cream, ice cream, custard or just straight up.

Serves 6–8
Preparation time: 15 minutes
Cooking time: 30 minutes

butter, for greasing
320g/11½oz/1 sheet of ready-rolled
   sweet shortcrust pastry
2 ripe pears, quartered, cored
   and sliced lengthways into 5mm
   (¼ inch) thick slices
icing sugar, for dusting

Frangipane
200g (7oz) butter
200g (7oz) caster sugar
2 eggs
200g (7oz) ground almonds

Preheat your oven to 160°C fan/350°F/gas mark 4. Grease a 25cm (10 inch) pie dish with butter.

To make the frangipane, cream together the butter and sugar in a mixing bowl until pale. Slowly add the eggs, then add the ground almonds.

Line the prepared pie dish with the pastry. Put a sheet of baking paper on top and fill with baking beans or rice. Bake until the exposed edges start to turn golden – this should take about 10 minutes. Take out and remove the paper and beans, then bake for a further 6 minutes, or until the base is golden brown too.

Spoon the frangipane mix into the pastry case and spread it out evenly. Lay the slices of pear around, overlapping them slightly. Bake for a further 20 minutes, until the frangipane is set and golden. Allow to cool before taking out of the case.

Dust with icing sugar to finish.

Cherry & almond pie (*pictured overleaf*) You can't beat a cherry pie. It's the smell that gets me; when you walk into someone's house and smell that pie baking – it's heaven. Almonds are cherries' best friends and here I incorporate them into the custard so it's a very subtle flavour.

Serves 6
Preparation time: 20 minutes
Cooking time: 35 minutes

butter, for greasing
5 tablespoons cherry jam
2 tablespoons caster sugar,
  plus extra to serve
1kg (2lb 4oz) fresh cherries, stones
  removed, halved
milk, for brushing
caster sugar, for dusting

For the pastry
250g (9oz) plain flour
90g (3¼oz) icing sugar
125g (4½oz) butter
1 vanilla pod, seeds only
1 small egg
(or use 200g/7oz/2 sheets
  of ready-rolled sweet
  shortcrust pastry)

Almond custard
225ml (8fl oz) almond milk
225ml (8fl oz) double cream
50ml (2fl oz) Ameretto
3 egg yolks
50g (1½oz) caster sugar

To make the pastry, mix all the ingredients together until smooth, cover with clingfilm and allow to rest for 30 minutes.

Preheat your oven to 160°C fan/350°F/gas mark 4. Grease a 25cm (10 inch) pie dish with butter.

In a saucepan, heat the jam with the sugar and bring to the boil. Take off the heat, add the cherries and stir through. Allow to get cold.

Cut the pastry in half and roll out each piece a little bigger than your pie dish. Line the pie dish with 1 sheet of the pastry. Pour in the cherry mixture, then cover with the other sheet of pastry. Using a fork, pinch the sides together so it is all well sealed. Cut a few slits in the top of the pastry to let the steam out while the pie is cooking. Using a pastry brush, brush the top with milk, then sprinkle over some caster sugar. Bake for 30 minutes – the pastry should be golden brown.

In the meantime, make the custard. Heat the milk, cream and Amaretto in a pan. Whisk the egg yolks and sugar together in a large bowl. Once the milk and cream have boiled, slowly pour on to the yolk mix and stir well. Return it to a low heat, stirring constantly until it thickens, taking care not to scramble the eggs. Take off the heat and pass through a sieve. Set aside.

When the pie is ready, let cool for 20 minutes, then sprinkle with caster sugar and dish up with a good jug of custard. This is equally good served hot or cold.

Queen of Puddings I don't see this British classic appearing on nearly as many menus as it should. With breadcrumbs to thicken the custard and a topping of jam and crunchy meringue, this is a truly gorgeous pudding. I've added a few Earl Grey tea bags to give a subtle background flavour.

Serves 6
Preparation time: 30 minutes
Cooking time: 40 minutes

4 tablespoons strawberry jam
caster sugar, for dusting
butter, for greasing

Meringue
4 egg whites
200g (7oz) caster sugar

Custard
500ml (18fl oz) milk
50g (1¾oz) caster sugar
2 Earl Grey tea bags
1 vanilla pod, seeds only
100g (3½oz) white breadcrumbs
1 lemon, zest only
4 egg yolks, beaten

Preheat your oven to 160°C fan/350°F/gas mark 4. Grease a 25cm (10 inch) pie dish.

To make the custard, put the milk, sugar, tea bags and vanilla seeds into a medium saucepan and bring to the boil. Reduce the heat to a simmer and leave for 5 minutes to extract the flavour from the tea.

Remove and discard the tea bags, then turn off the heat and stir in the breadcrumbs and lemon zest. Allow to sit for 10–15 minutes. The breadcrumbs will absorb lots of the milk and swell. Stir in the egg yolks, then spoon the mixture into the greased pie dish. Bake for 25 minutes, or until set.

Meanwhile, make the meringue. Whisk the egg whites until stiff, then, continuing to whisk, add the sugar.

When the custard is ready, take it out of the oven and spread the jam evenly over the top. You may want to heat up the jam a little to make this easier.

Now spoon or pipe the meringue evenly over the whole pie. Sprinkle evenly with caster sugar, then bake for 15 minutes. The meringue should be golden brown, the sugar caramelizing to give a nice crunch.

Custard-soaked brioche pudding, baked plums, clotted cream

Custard and brioche; what's not to love? If plums aren't around, try using apples, berries or even roasted pineapple with a splash of rum.

Serves 4
Preparation time: 30 minutes
Cooking time: 30 minutes

4 slices of brioche, approx. 2cm
  (¾ inch) thick
6 plums, halved and stones
  removed
caster sugar, for sprinkling
sunflower oil, for cooking
4 tablespoons clotted cream

Custard
225ml (8fl oz) milk
225ml (8fl oz) double cream
3 egg yolks
50g (1¾oz) sugar

Caramel
125g (4½oz) caster sugar
1 tablespoon water
25g (1oz) butter
75ml (2½fl oz) double cream

To make the custard, heat the milk and cream in a pan. Meanwhile whisk the egg yolks and sugar together. Once the milk and cream have boiled, slowly pour on to the yolk mix and stir well. Normally you'd return this to the heat to cook and thicken, but we will keep it at this stage, as the eggs will get cooked after soaking into the brioche.

Pour the custard into a baking tray, and add the slices of brioche. Push down with your fingers so the custard soaks in. Leave on the side while you prepare the plums.

Preheat your oven to 180°C fan/400°F/gas mark 6. On a baking sheet lined with baking paper, lay out the plums, cut side up, and sprinkle each one with some caster sugar. Bake for 15 minutes, so the sugar caramelizes and the fruit softens. Take them out, but leave the oven on.

To make the caramel, put the sugar into a saucepan with a tablespoon of water and cook over a medium heat until it becomes a light brown caramel colour. Turn off the heat and stir in the butter and cream. Set aside for later.

Heat a frying pan on a medium heat and add a splash of sunflower oil. Take each slice of brioche out of the custard, allowing the excess to fall off. Carefully fry each slice until golden brown, and then pop on to a tray. Once all 4 slices are cooked, coat each one in caster sugar, put back on the tray and bake for 10–12 minutes. The slices should be caramelized on the outside and have a slight crust, but be soft in the middle.

To serve, top each slice with a couple of the roasted plums, a tablespoon of clotted cream and a drizzle of caramel sauce.

Plum jam roly-poly, Amaretto custard

I like to use almond milk for this retro British classic. It gives a rounder flavour, which is further highlighted by the Amaretto custard.

Serves 4
Preparation time: 20 minutes
Cooking time: 50 minutes

Sponge
220g (8oz) self-raising flour
40g (1½oz) butter, plus extra for
  greasing
1 vanilla pod, seeds only
40g (1½oz) shredded suet
120ml (4fl oz) almond milk
80g (2¾oz) plum jam

Amaretto custard
225ml (8fl oz) almond milk
40ml (1½fl oz) amaretto
225ml (8fl oz) double cream
3 egg yolks
45g (1½oz) caster sugar

Preheat the oven to 180°C fan/400°F/Gas Mark 6.

In a food processor, combine the flour, butter and vanilla seeds. Add the suet into the mixture but incorporate by hand, not using the mixer. Gradually add the almond milk and combine until a dough is formed.

On a floured surface, roll out the dough to a square roughly 1cm (½ inch) thick. Spread the jam all over, stopping short of one edge. Butter a sheet of foil that is slightly bigger than the dough, then carefully lift the dough on to the foil. Use the foil to help you roll up the dough, finishing at the end with no jam. Wrap it up in the foil loosely, to allow for a little rising, then transfer to a baking tray.

Take a roasting dish, pour in some water and pop this on to the bottom shelf of the oven to provide some moisture. Put the baking tray with the jam roly-poly on the shelf above and bake for 50 minutes.

Meanwhile, make the custard. Heat the almond milk, amaretto and cream in a pan. In a large bowl, whisk the egg yolks and sugar together. Once the milk and cream are steaming hot, slowly pour on to the yolk mix and stir well. Return to a low heat, stirring constantly until it thickens, taking care not to scramble the egg yolks. Take the pan off the heat and pass the custard through a sieve. Set aside for later.

Take the roly-poly out of the oven and allow to rest for 10 minutes. Then slice and serve, with a jug of custard on the side.

Cherry clafoutis The French have given us some stunning desserts and this classic is up there as one of my favourites. It's kind of a baked fruit batter, with the fruits submerged and all baked together; the perfect end to a Sunday lunch, and it's great with ice cream too.

Serves 6
Preparation time: 1 hour
Cooking time: 30 minutes

100g (3½oz) caster sugar, plus
    extra for sprinkling
50ml (2fl oz) kirsch
500g (1lb 2oz) cherries, stones
    removed, halved
30g (1oz) butter, plus extra for
    greasing
3 eggs
1 vanilla pod, seeds only
20g (¾oz) plain flour
75ml (2½fl oz) milk
100ml (3½fl oz) double cream
2 tablespoons crème fraîche,
    to serve

Preheat the oven to 180°C fan/400°F/gas mark 6. Grease a 23cm (9 inch) baking dish with butter, then sprinkle with caster sugar all over. Tap off the excess.

Bring the kirsch and 20g (¾oz) of the sugar to the boil in a small pan, then the pan take off the heat and add the cherries. Stir through and allow to sit for 1 hour.

To make the clafoutis batter, melt the butter in a small pan. In a mixing bowl, whisk the eggs, 80g (2¾oz) of the sugar and the vanilla seeds until thick and creamy. While still whisking, add the flour, then the milk, the cream and finally the melted butter. Fold in the cherries and their juices.

Pour the mixture into the baking dish and sprinkle a layer of caster sugar on top. Bake for 30 minutes, or until the top is golden brown and a skewer inserted in the centre comes out clean. Serve with a spoonful of crème fraîche on each plate.

Apple, ricotta & honey muffins with sesame seed crunch

I like to make these wholesome muffins on a Sunday so we have breakfast to go during the week. There's very little sugar in them so they're not too naughty…

Makes 12
Preparation time: 15 minutes
Cooking time: 15 minutes

butter, for greasing
125g (4½oz) plain flour
125g (4½oz) wholemeal flour
2 teaspoons baking powder
1 teaspoon ground cinnamon
2 eggs, beaten
2 apples, grated
150g (5½oz) ricotta cheese
60g (2¼oz) raisins
3 tablespoons honey
60g (2¼oz) butter, melted
100ml (3½fl oz) apple juice

Sesame crunch
3 tablespoons honey
40g (1½oz) sesame seeds

Preheat the oven to 180°C fan/400°F/gas mark 6. Grease the holes of a 12-hole muffin tin with butter.

Put the flours, baking powder and cinnamon into a mixing bowl and combine. In a separate bowl, mix together the egg, grated apple, ricotta, raisins and honey. Add the wet mix to the dry mix, and stir in the melted butter and apple juice.

To make the sesame crunch, mix the honey and sesame seeds together.

Spoon the muffin mix into the prepared tin, drizzling a spoonful of the sesame crunch over each one. Bake for 15 minutes.

When risen and golden, allow to cool for 5 minutes before carefully turning out.

DRINKS

First, I'm not, by any stretch of the imagination, a mixologist. I do, however, love all drinks. From cocktails to hard shakes – I'm not shy about having a crack at them at home. Being a chef and not a bar expert, the drinks recipes in this chapter are simple and focus more on the food side of things, especially vegetables.

I can't claim all the credit, though; I had to ask an old friend for help writing these recipes. I first met Francesco Pistone back in 2002, during my apprenticeship at 1 Lombard Street, where he was managing the bars. We struck up a friendship immediately, sharing a respect for tradition and our opinions on the way things should be, while also both having a passion for innovation. Francesco is so humble, but so bloody good at what he does. I have a huge amount of respect for him and consider him a dear friend.

Breakfast smoothies

Smoothies for breakfast have always been a thing but now they seem to be more popular than ever – maybe due to the wave of new high-powered machines available. The idea is that smoothies provide a healthy boost to get your day started right, but that doesn't mean they need to be boring or bland. In the following recipes I've taken familiar flavour combinations and "blended" them to create new and exciting ways to get you up in the morning. For each recipe there is, naturally, a naughty suggestion, should you fancy a treat…

PBJ

Serves 2
Preparation time: 2 minutes

1 banana
1 tablespoon peanut butter
a handful of strawberries, hulled
200ml (7fl oz) almond milk
a handful of ice cubes
1 tablespoon strawberry jam

Naughty – add a scoop of toffee or
  vanilla ice cream

Roughly slice the banana directly into a blender. Add the strawberries to the blender along with the remaining ingredients. Blitz until smooth. Pour into 2 glasses and serve.

Apple pie

Serves 2
Preparation time: 4 minutes

1 apple
½ banana
a pinch of ground cinnamon,
  plus extra to garnish
200ml (7fl oz) hazelnut milk
a handful of ice cubes
a handful of Granola
  (see page 100)

Naughty – add a scoop of salted
  caramel ice cream

Peel and core the apple, chop into 1cm (½in) cubes and add to a blender. Roughly slice the banana directly into the blender and add the remaining ingredients. Blitz until smooth. Pour into 2 glasses and serve with a sprinkling of ground cinnamon on top.

Banoffee

Serves 2
Preparation time: 2 minutes

1 banana
1 tablespoon Greek yoghurt
200ml (7fl oz) milk
4 dates, pitted
1 tablespoon honey
a small piece of dark chocolate,
   for grating

Naughty – add a scoop of toffee
   ice cream

Roughly slice the banana directly into a blender. Add the yoghurt, milk, dates and honey (and ice cream, if you're feeling naughty). Blitz until smooth. Pour into 2 glasses and serve with a grating of dark chocolate on top.

Peach melba

Serves 2
Preparation time: 5 minutes

1 ripe peach
a handful of raspberries
a handful of ice cubes
200ml (7fl oz) almond milk
a pinch of flaked almonds, toasted,
   to garnish

Naughty – add a scoop of vanilla
   ice cream

Peel the peach, then roughly chop and add it into a blender along with the raspberries, ice cubes and almond milk (and ice cream, if you're feeling naughty). Blitz until smooth. Pour into 2 glasses and serve with a sprinkling of flaked almonds on top.

Overleaf, from left to right: Apple Pie; PBJ; Banoffee; Peach Melba

Vege-tails Vegetables are my latest obsession; I'm using them in all kinds of ways in my menus at the restaurant, including desserts. With so many amazing drinks popping up in bars across the country, I felt inspired to play with them using our friends from the earth. These recipes are simple, but tasty, and are technically one of your five-a-day… You'll need sugar syrup for some of these recipes. To make it at home, the ratio is 1 part water to 2 parts sugar.

English garden daiquiri

Serves 2
Preparation time: 2 minutes

50g (1¾oz) poached rhubarb
100g (3½oz) cucumber, peeled
  and deseeded
2 strawberries, hulled
seeds from 1 vanilla pod
25ml (1fl oz) gin
25ml (1fl oz) sugar syrup
finely grated zest of 1 lemon
2 handfuls of crushed ice

Put the rhubarb and cucumber into a blender along with the remaining ingredients. Blitz until smooth. Pour into 2 glasses and serve.

Fennel & Lemon Bellini

Serves 2
Preparation time: 5 minutes

110ml (3¾fl oz) Prosecco
15ml Fennel & Dill Syrup (see right)
lemon peel, to garnish

Pour the Prosecco into 2 glasses, then add the Fennel & Dill Syrup very slowly. Stir very briefly. Garnish each with a lemon twist.

Fennel & dill syrup Put 400ml (14fl oz) sugar syrup into a blender with 120g (4¼oz) fresh fennel, roughly chopped, a pinch of fresh dill and 12 fennel seeds. Blitz for 1 minute at high speed. Strain the syrup twice through muslin. Pour into a sterilized bottle and store it in the fridge. Shake before using.

Carrot Aperol
For this drink I have always used home-squeezed carrot juice, made using a juicer, but it could work with any good brand of shop-bought carrot juice.

Serves 2
Preparation time: 1 minute

50ml (2fl oz) carrot juice
35ml (1¼fl oz) Aperol
20ml (¾fl oz) pisco
20ml (¾fl oz) fresh lime juice
20ml (¾fl oz) sugar syrup
  (see page 210)
handful of ice cubes

Shake everything together in a cocktail shaker with ice. Strain into 2 cocktail glasses and serve.

Red pepper margarita

Serves 2
Preparation time: 1 minute

60ml (2fl oz) Thyme & Lemon
  Syrup (see below)
100ml (3½fl oz) Red Pepper-
  infused Tequila (see below)
45ml (3 tablespoons) fresh lime
  juice
a pinch of salt

Shake everything together in a cocktail shaker with ice. Strain into 2 cocktail glasses and serve.

Thyme & lemon syrup
Makes enough for 6–8 cocktails. In a pan on a medium heat, bring 180ml (6fl oz) water to the boil. Add 175g (6oz) caster sugar and stir gently to dissolve. Add 4 slices of lemon and 4 sprigs of fresh thyme and allow to infuse for 5 minutes. Strain and leave to cool.

Red pepper-infused Tequila
Makes 500ml (18fl oz). Put 500ml (18fl oz) tequila blanco into a sterilized jar with 130g (4¾oz) red pepper, deseeded and cut into 5mm (¼ inch) strips. Put the jar into a cool, dark cupboard and leave to infuse for at least 3 hours and up to 24 hours. Double strain through cheesecloth or muslin before serving.

Bloody Mary As far as hangover cures go a Bloody Mary has to be the most successful. I'm not quite sure what it is about it: the spice, the tomato juice, the little top up of vodka to lure you into a false sense of freshness – whatever it is, it works. Another great thing about a Bloody Mary is its versatility. Whether adding a savoury element, or totally mixing it up with beetroot and dill, you can really play around with the flavours.

Bloody Mary base

Serves 2
Preparation time: 5 minutes

175ml (6fl oz) tomato juice
freshly ground black pepper
a pinch of sea salt flakes
a pinch of celery salt
3 dashes of Tabasco
6 dashes of Worcestershire sauce
½ lemon, juice only
a pinch of fennel seeds
50ml (2fl oz) vodka
ice cubes

Stir all the ingredients together with ice. Pour into 2 glasses and serve.

Beetroot bloody Mary

Serves 2
Preparation time: 5 minutes

50ml (2fl oz) London dry gin
200ml (7fl oz) Beetroot Juice Mix
  (see below)
a squeeze of fresh lemon juice
a pinch of celery salt
ice cubes
small sprig of fresh dill, chopped,
  to garnish

Put all the ingredients, except the dill, into a jug, add ice, and stir. Pour into 2 highball glasses or large wine glasses, and serve garnished with the dill.

Beetroot juice mix (Makes 200ml/7fl oz)
Put 4 ready-cooked beetroots, roughly chopped, into a blender along with a 2cm (1 inch) piece of horseradish, grated, 1 celery stick, chopped, 100ml (3½fl oz) water and 1 tablespoon crème fraîche. Blitz until smooth, then strain through cheesecloth or muslin before using.
If you prefer, you can buy good beetroot juice and blend it with the horseradish, celery, water and crème fraîche.

Hard shakes
Life is all about balance and these are my response to the healthy breakfast smoothies on pages 206–7. Hard shakes are a little naughty, certainly tasty, and again, play on familiar flavours that I think work great as an indulgent shake. They make the perfect toast for a brunch get together.

Banana & rum

Serves 2
Preparation time: 5 minutes

1 banana
25ml (1fl oz) rum
1 scoop of vanilla ice cream
100ml (3½fl oz) coconut milk
1 tablespoon desiccated coconut
grated nutmeg, to garnish

Roughly slice the banana directly into a blender and add the remaining ingredients, except the nutmeg. Blitz until smooth. Pour into 2 glasses and serve with a grating of nutmeg on top.

Breakfast espresso martini

Serves 2
Preparation time: 5 minutes

1 double espresso
50ml (2fl oz) vodka
4 teaspoons coffee liqueur
1 scoop of vanilla ice cream
100ml (3½fl oz) almond milk
2 amaretti biscuits

Put all the ingredients, except the amaretti biscuits, into a blender. Blitz until smooth. Pour into 2 glasses and serve with an amaretti biscuit crumbled on top.

Strawberries 'n' cream

Serves 2
Preparation time: 5 minutes

1 handful of strawberries, hulled
1 scoop of vanilla ice cream
25ml (1fl oz) sweet vermouth
25ml (1fl oz) vodka
2 fresh mint leaves, finely sliced

Put all the ingredients into a blender. Blitz until smooth. Pour into 2 glasses and serve.

Baileys & cookie crumble

Serves 2
Preparation time: 2 minutes

50ml (2fl oz) Baileys
2 Oreo cookies
1 scoop of vanilla ice cream
100ml (3½fl oz) hazelnut milk

Put all the ingredients into a blender. Blitz until smooth. Pour into 2 glasses and serve.

Index

A

almond
  & cherry pie 189, 191
  & chocolate spread 15
  milk 15, 196, 206–7, 216
  & pear frangipane tart 188, 190
Aperol, carrot 212, 213
apple
  maple-roasted, with French toast 185
  pie smoothie 206, 208
  ricotta & honey muffins 200–1
  toffee apple pancakes with granola crumble 100, 102
artichokes, fried, with harissa mayo 170–1
avocado 18, 21, 54, 88

B

bacon
  in Colcann-bac-on 76–7
  crumbs 165
  & eggy bread sarnie 52–3
    in hash 65
  jam, with pancakes & runny eggs 94–5
  parsnip & apple chop 69, 71
  with potato waffle 117
  with roast chicken 156
  smoky, sloppy Joes 134–5
  ultimate grilled sandwich 114
bagel, "eggs Benedict", salt beef & mustard hollandaise 38–9
Baileys & cookie crumble hard shake 218, 219
banana
  bread French toast with maple-roasted apples 184–5
  & rum hard shake 216, 217
  in smoothies 206, 207

beans
  black, in Feijoada 154
  Indian-spiced 30–1
beef
  bubble & squeak 72–3
  corned, hash 74–5
  Harissa bolognese with baked eggs 50–1
  patty melt 128
  roast, & mustard toast 24–5
beetroot 26–7, 214
Bellini, fennel & lemon 210, 211
bhaji, Scotch egg 120–1
black pudding hash 66
Bloody Mary 214, 215
blue cheese 112–13, 156
bread
  brioche pudding 194
  croutons 175
  rye, Reuben 16–17
  sourdough 18–33
  see also toast
brioche pudding with custard, plums & clotted cream 194–5
broad beans, in salad 175
broccoli
  in hash 65, 73
  & poached eggs 40, 43
Brussels sprouts 68, 70
bubble & squeak 72–3
butternut squash 92–3, 172–3

C

cabbage, in hash 65
Camembert, baked, with cheese straws 122–3
carrots
  carrot Aperol 212, 213
  roasted 164, 167, 176
cauliflower, curried
  boiled eggs & coconut crumble 60–1

in hash 68, 70
chard 169
Cheddar 52–3, 54–5
cheese
  polenta with leftover meat stew 118–19
  with potato waffle throw-down 117
  straws with baked Camembert 122–3
  on toast 112
  ultimate grilled sandwich 114–15
  see also type of cheese
cherry
  & almond pie 189, 191
  clafoutis 198–9
chicken
  congee, ginger, spring onion & runny eggs 142–3
  harissa, feta & sweet potato hash 80–1
  roast, on potato, bacon & mushroom ragoût 156–7
  & waffles 132–3
chickpea pancakes 92–3
chocolate
  & almond spread 15, 106
  strawberry, almond & biscuit crumble pancake wraps 106–7
chorizo
  breakfast tacos 130–1
  in Feijoada 154–5
  with sweetcorn & sweet potato pancakes 91
  with Turkish eggs 48–9
clafoutis, cherry 198–9
cocktails 210–15
coconut milk 60, 216
coconut pancakes with rum roasted pineapple 104–5
coffee, espresso hard shake 216, 217
Colcann-bac-on 76–7

Acknowledgements

When I wrote my first book, *Duck & Waffle Recipes & Stories*, it truly hit home just how many people are involved when writing a book, and makes you realize this is the most important page you'll write. That said, I always miss someone, so if I did, I apologise now.

To all at Octopus: I'd like to say thank you for believing in me to produce another book. To Alison, Caroline, Sybella, Juliette and all, thank you.

The phenomenally talented photographer, and good friend of mine, Anders. Thanks for going through all this again with me! I hope we fed you enough…

Liz Belton for making everything look gorgeous and for keeping us in line.

To Holly, for your unwavering support throughout.

To all the staff at Duck & Waffle for putting up with me randomly cooking egg-based dishes in the middle of service and generally being a nuisance.

For Shimon, my boss, thank you for letting me do this – I'm very fortunate to work for someone who understands creativity and passion like you do. You didn't question this project once and I truly appreciate that.

Last but by no means least my best friend, and Head Chef at Duck & Waffle, Tom who was there every day on the shoots, cooking, styling and organizing like no other. We've known each other and worked together for 16 years now and that makes me feel very lucky. Thank you Cheffie.